CREATING & CRAFTING
DOLLS

Patterns, Techniques, and Inspiration for Making Cloth Dolls

Eloise Piper & Mary Dilligan

CHILTON BOOK COMPANY, RADNOR, PENNSYLVANIA

Book design by Eloise Piper

Illustrations by Eloise Piper

Photographs by Ed Kessler, Product Shots, Carlsbad, CA 92009

Give Me Color! is a registered trademark of Matthew Thomas Designs. All Give Me Color!™ products, patterns for Give Me Color!™ products, and the patterns included in this book are copyrighted by Matthew Thomas Designs. Information about supplies used in this book is available from Matthew Thomas Designs, 4235 Arden Way, San Diego, CA 92103.

Library of Congress Cataloging in Publication Data

Piper, Eloise.
  Creating & crafting dolls: patterns, techniques, and inspirations for making cloth dolls: featuring Give me color! doll patterns / Eloise Piper & Mary Dilligan.
    p. cm. —(Craft kaleidoscope)
  Includes index.
  ISBN 0-8019-8524-2
  1. Dollmaking. 2. Cloth dolls. 3. Doll clothes—Patterns. I. Dilligan, Mary. II. Title. III. Title: Creating and crafting dolls. IV. Series.
TT175.P57 1994   93-45404
745.592'21—dc20   CIP

1 2 3 4 5 6 7 8 9 0   3 2 1 0 9 8 7 6 5 4

To Carolyn, Megan, Tom, and Matt,
and in memory of Aaron and Booth.

CONTENTS

FOREWORD

My two earliest memories of sewing happened at my mother's feet as she sewed on our old Singer: stringing buttons and dressing dolls in crude T-shirts. I remember being totally absorbed in these activities, with no sense of time passing, and having a feeling of glee when the dolls were dressed in something I—I!—had made.

Today my life is full of responsibilities and deadlines. Happily, though, I've discovered that I can recreate that floating sense of gleeful no-time by sewing. I become temporarily free of the earth, alive in the moment. I especially love to intersperse making little dolls with other, more ambitious sewing projects.

Something magical happens when you make a cloth doll. Even if you're starting with purchased blank dolls and you make them all in the same day, each will turn out different. This continues to delight me. A slight variation in eyebrow tilt, placement of irises, or lip fullness gives birth to a unique little being.

I confess to having had a certain intimidation about painting faces. I know from experience how cock-eyed a face can look when it doesn't conform to certain relationships between eyes, nose, ears, and mouth. That's what I particularly like about Mary and Ellie's book. They lead us step-by-step through face painting and embroidering. I also like all the ideas for embellishing, recycling fabrics, using pens and dyes, varying hair.

I look at each little blank doll and say silently, "Tell me what you want to become." The world slows down. I begin to float in no-time. And the doll and I astonish ourselves by being and becoming. ◼

Robbie Fanning, Series Editor

INTRODUCTION

Dollmaking is a fascinating craft. The transformation of bits of fabric, dabs of paint, and snippets of floss into a lively little person is truly a magical process. With a bit of time and a sense of adventure, you can master the skills you need to create and craft wonderful dolls.

We are women who have always loved dolls, and we became dollmakers through the process of making lots of dolls. Our dolls have evolved—from early dolls that sometimes seem crude to the more detailed, subtly crafted dolls that we created after months of experience, much trial and error, and a great deal of pleasure. Our own skills developed as we discovered new materials and experimented with new techniques.

We have been working together for several years. Mary developed the Give Me Color! line of presewn craft items, and Ellie designed and edited four Give Me Color! books with techniques and designs for fabric painting. The dollmaking projects were hands-down favorites, especially Ellie's simple penned dolls in *Fresh Flowers*. Readers were particularly enthusiastic about her drawing of the facial features and her techniques for planning and positioning the doll's face.

From this response we realized that many crafters are intimidated by blank bodies and faces; they want to know how to put on a face and create a personality and they want suggestions on what to use for hair and how to make clothes. We saw that the readers liked the mix-and-match design elements in *Fresh Flowers*, so we developed this presentation into a complete dollmaking book.

Ellie brought her fine-arts background and painting experience to these simple, little dolls. As she prepared dolls for magazine articles and trade-show displays, she experimented with the many different materials available in crafts stores. Using a variety of media—some familiar to her, some not—she developed several series of doll faces. Although she changed the features in size and varied the placement and coloring, she always achieved a facial unity. The eyes and the nose and the mouth all go together and the colors are harmonious.

Mary became involved with the embellishment at a much later stage. She was delighted to see how other craftspeople transformed her Give Me Color! dolls, and she gathered images in her mind of the kinds of dolls she would like to create. But she was intimidated by faces, as she remembered some of her early regrettable efforts. When a quantity of 12" dolls had to be completed, however, she discovered that by following Ellie's face technique she could make dolls that looked good. As she improved with experience, Mary contributed her hand-sewing abilities to create dolls with embroidered features. Take this confession as proof positive that *you*, too, can apply faces to dolls and that practice leads to confidence in your abilities.

Although we work together, we create dolls in different ways. Ellie rarely chooses to sew a doll body. She either uses a ready-made Give Me Color! doll or appeals to her sewing friends to stitch a doll from a special fabric. As Ellie looks at the blank doll she images a character in her mind and then gathers all of her supplies. Her experience as an artist gives her the ability to choose colors with confidence and her creativity enables her to transform unlikely materials as well as traditional fabrics and trims into the object of her imagination.

Mary begins a doll project by choosing materials she finds appealing, perhaps a linen with a lovely edging or a fabric remnant. The materials are clues to a theme or a style, but she doesn't know right away how she is going to put them all together. It is only as she cuts and sews that it becomes apparent how the outfit is going to be constructed and what else is necessary to complete the doll's design.

The creative process will be different for you, just as it is for each of us, but no matter how you approach dollmaking, you can't go wrong. You are free to be inventive and experiment with new colors and materials—the process, not the product, is the most delightful part of dollmaking. Relax and enjoy the stitching and painting. Let any unanticipated results spark your creativity; see how a dot here or a few stitches there can transform surprises into assets.

This book is for crafters, artists, sewers, dollmakers, moms, and grandmoms. It is for people who enjoy the creative process and who want to learn specific techniques for dollmaking. In this book, we take a practical and flexible approach to dollmaking. We construct our dolls from readily available art, craft, and sewing materials. Because the bodies are simple, generic shapes, our focus is on the elements that bring the doll to life. Using our easy-to-follow instructions and some practice, anybody can create imaginative, expressive dolls from a few basic supplies.

You have a unique set of skills and talents that will increase as you become a dollmaker. To develop your skills and to encourage your creativity, we present projects for making playable dolls suitable for young children. Through planning, designing, and creating simple dolls, you will master the techniques shown here and gain confidence in your dollmaking abilities, and you will also have a loving gift to share.

Begin by making a doll body from the patterns and instructions in Chapter 1. These same bodies can be purchased as 12", 5$^1/2$", and 3$^1/2$" Give Me Color! ready-made blank dolls in your local crafts or fabric store. In Chapters 1 and 2 you will learn to choose fabrics for bodies and clothes, select yarns and trims for hair, and embroider faces and garments. In Chapter 2 also we teach you how to assemble the essential art and craft supplies and how to use them to apply skin tones and faces to your dolls. Chapters 3 and 4 include plenty of traditional patterns to create imaginative wardrobes for your dolls and instructions on how to create patterns from circles and rectangles. As you design clothing styles, you are encouraged to experiment with recycled linens and knits.

Familiarize yourself with all of the features of this book. Look at the photographs as inspiration for combining colors and fabrics, as well as for suggestions for face and garment design. Study Ellie's delightful ink drawings to get ideas for additional outfits, hairstyles, and facial expressions.

Use the index to match materials and techniques to instructional diagrams, photos, and directions.

Our goal is to teach you basic dollmaking techniques, to introduce you to supplies we enjoy using, and to share with you the many dolls we have created using these materials and processes. Most of our dolls are playable dolls for children, but the techniques can be used on decorative dolls and on bodies of your own design.

Dollmaking is a wonderful way to rediscover the richness of your own personal creativity. We encourage you to make many variations of dolls as you gain confidence in your abilities. You will find that your eyes will see more colors and your mind will imagine more faces as your hands become more skilled at creating and crafting dolls.

1 · DOLL BODIES

PATTERNS AND INSTRUCTIONS
FOR GIVE ME COLOR! DOLLS

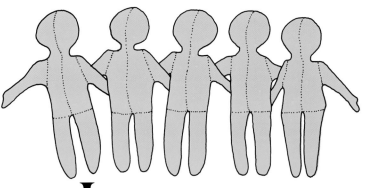

In this chapter you will learn to make the 12", 5$\frac{1}{2}$", and 3$\frac{1}{2}$" Give Me Color! doll bodies used for the projects in this book. You will first gather your tools and materials and then transfer the patterns from the book to paper patterns or templates. You will choose fabrics, thread, and stuffing to complete the body for your first doll project. We like these dolls because their simple, unassuming shapes give you a lot of options for creating and crafting doll characters as you develop your dollmaking skills. As you cut and sew each body, begin to imagine the delightful playmates and companions you are about to create.

If you prefer, you can purchase ready-made Give Me Color! dolls from your local crafts or fabric store. But whether you make or buy your blank doll, you'll notice that each one is amazingly different. Elements such as the cut of the fabric, the stitching of the seams, and the manner of stuffing can lead to a doll that is slender with a thin neck and delicate head or one that is chunky with plump features. Enjoy the individuality of your doll, whether it is a purchased doll or one you've sewn from the following instructions.

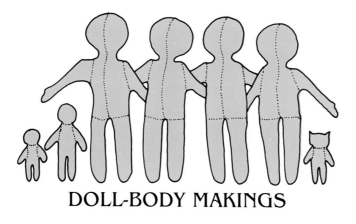

DOLL-BODY MAKINGS

Here are the supplies needed to cut out, sew, and stuff doll bodies. You may find many of them among your own sewing and craft materials.

FABRICS

Doll-body fabric takes a great deal of punishment as it is stitched and clipped, turned and stuffed. An excellent choice is mediumweight, tightly woven cotton. Look for a smooth cotton with a high thread count and one which doesn't fray easily. Pima cotton has long, strong fibers and is wonderfully sturdy and supple. Its soft, even surface is perfect for paint, pen, and embroidery embellishment.

Each fabric contributes to the unique character of your doll, adding texture to your design, as well as color and pattern. As you become experienced, be adventurous with knits, velvets, suedes, and terry cloths. Knits may stretch as you stuff the body, particularly on the crosswise grain. This often causes the doll's arms to become long as its neck and body become pudgy. Sometimes we pull knitted fabrics on the crosswise grain and iron them before laying out the pattern. Remember these characteristics when you begin to combine several fabrics in one doll body.

You have many choices for the doll's skin color. Solids in pinks, peaches, and browns are traditional favorites, but also consider small dots, tiny all-over prints, and plaids. Match all directional patterns and be on the lookout for unexpected designs that may appear at the face seam.

You may want to wash fabrics to shrink them and to remove sizing, which can prevent fabric from accepting dyes. The instructions for most fabric paints and pens recommend that the products be used on natural fabrics that have been washed. We suggest, however, that you test your fabric to determine if you want to prewash it. We have found that sizing often gives cotton fabric a good surface on which to draw fine lines and to paint crisp areas. Color on a scrap of the doll fabric, then wash and dry it to see the results.

THREADS

Always machine sew doll bodies with strong thread that closely matches the doll-body fabric. The threads are particularly visible on the center seam of a well-stuffed body. If you cannot make a perfect match, a lighter rather than a darker thread is usually preferable. Keep your machine well maintained. Set it at 18 stitches per inch for the body construction seams and at 10 stitches per inch for topstitching. Use quilting thread to hand stitch the doll's opening.

STUFFINGS AND STUFFING TOOLS

Battings are available in polyester, cotton, and wool, but we prefer polyester fiberfill because it washes well and doesn't lump. We have found that some expensive polyester fills are silky and make squishy, soft toys. However, they may be more difficult to handle than the slightly coarser fills, which tend to be more economical.

The ideal stuffing tool has a blunt end to avoid poking a hole through the body and grabs the fill so that you can position it into the body's nooks and crannies. Stuffing tools are available in sewing and crafts stores, and many are designed to stuff tiny arms and fingers. Our projects are not so demanding, however, and we suggest you try knitting needles, chopsticks, or screwdrivers. An old, slightly twisted barbecue skewer has become our favorite stuffing tool.

PATTERNS & TEMPLATES

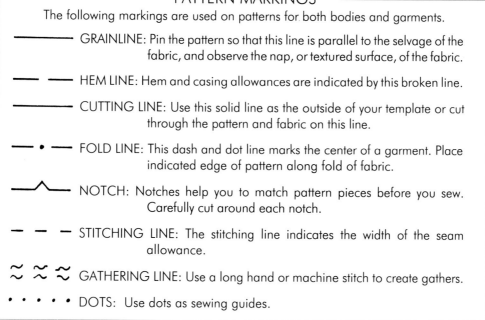

Keep a record of the patterns you use for your dolls and their clothes. With a pen, trace patterns on translucent grid paper by aligning the grainline of the pattern to the paper's grid line. Record all pattern markings and indicate the source of the pattern, the date, and the doll made. You will use these master patterns for many future projects. Trace a duplicate pattern to use for cutting out the fabric. If it becomes tattered from wear, you can trace a new one from your master.

Templates are sturdy forms that can be used to trace the pattern onto fabric if you are going to make multiple dolls. Cut templates from cardboard or from transparent plastic available at quilting supply shops. Transfer the pattern from the grid paper to the plastic or cardboard and cut out the template with sharp scissors or a craft knife.

Use a pencil to draw around the template on the wrong side of the doll-body fabric. Cut away all pencil lines to eliminate the possibility of smearing marks onto your project.

PATTERN MARKINGS

The following markings are used on patterns for both bodies and garments.

GRAINLINE: Pin the pattern so that this line is parallel to the selvage of the fabric, and observe the nap, or textured surface, of the fabric.

HEM LINE: Hem and casing allowances are indicated by this broken line.

CUTTING LINE: Use this solid line as the outside of your template or cut through the pattern and fabric on this line.

FOLD LINE: This dash and dot line marks the center of a garment. Place indicated edge of pattern along fold of fabric.

NOTCH: Notches help you to match pattern pieces before you sew. Carefully cut around each notch.

STITCHING LINE: The stitching line indicates the width of the seam allowance.

GATHERING LINE: Use a long hand or machine stitch to create gathers.

DOTS: Use dots as sewing guides.

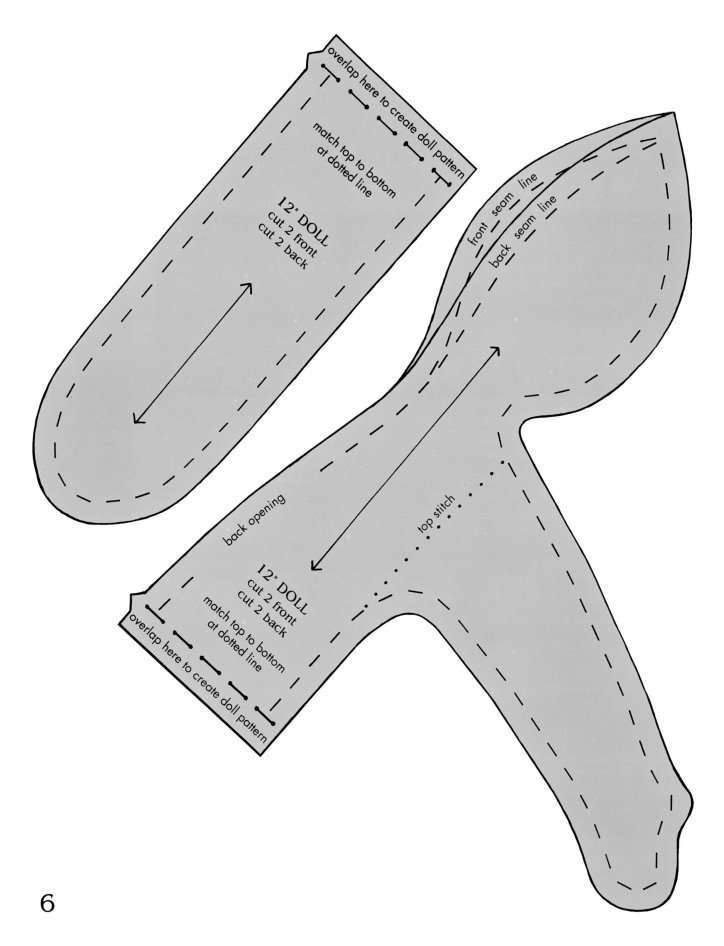

overlap here to create doll pattern

match top to bottom at dotted line

12" DOLL
cut 2 front
cut 2 back

front seam line

back seam line

back opening

top stitch

12" DOLL
cut 2 front
cut 2 back

match top to bottom at dotted line

overlap here to create doll pattern

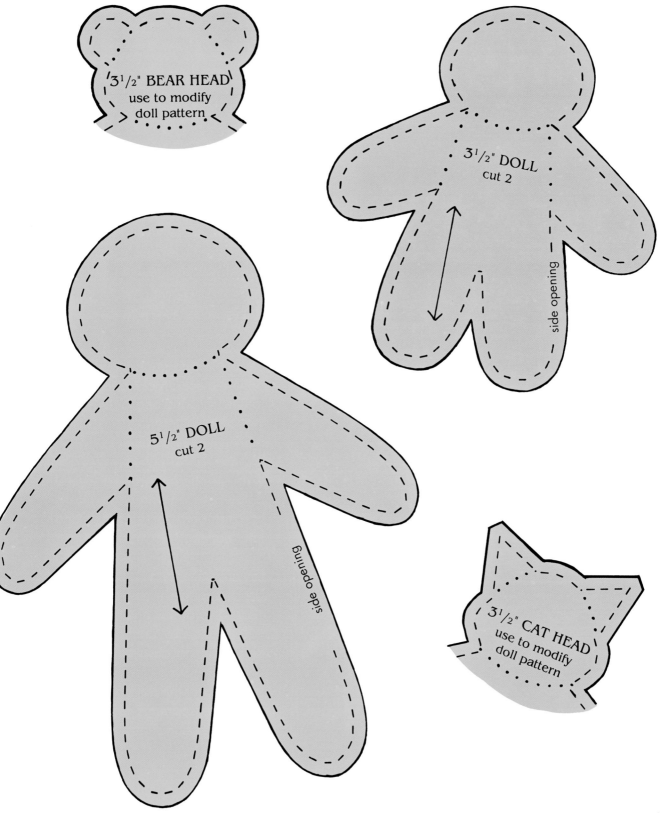

3¹/₂" BEAR HEAD
use to modify
doll pattern

3¹/₂" DOLL
cut 2

side opening

5¹/₂" DOLL
cut 2

side opening

3¹/₂" CAT HEAD
use to modify
doll pattern

12" DOLL INSTRUCTIONS

Use the 12" doll pattern for the First Dolls and Pieced Dolls in Chapter 3 and the Playmates in Chapter 4. You will transform this simple little doll with center front and center back seams into delightful characters of your imagination.

MATERIALS
$3/8$ yd. fabric, 3 oz. polyester stuffing

Assemble and trace the 12" doll pattern pieces. Make one pattern for the front and one for the back. Notice the difference! Record the markings on the patterns.

If you are going to make several dolls, make templates from plastic or cardboard for the back and front patterns.

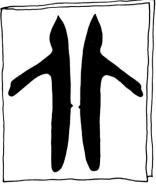

Lay out the pattern on your fabric. Use the diagram at left for purchased yardages and for fabrics with a one-way pattern or nap. Remember to always follow the lengthwise grain of the fabric for the height of the dolls and match plaids and patterns at both the center and side seams.

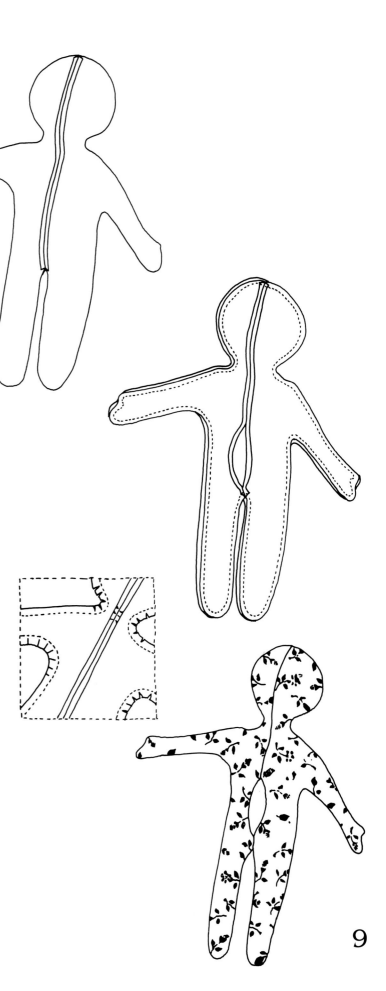

With right sides together, pin and stitch the front seam from the head to the notch. Pin and stitch the back seam from the head to the notch, leaving a 2" opening for stuffing. Clip seams at inside curves and finger-press seam open.

Pin and stitch the front to the back, right sides together, matching center seams at the head and crotch. Stitch around the body, using a $1/4$" seam allowance. Handle the pieces carefully so that you do not stretch the extremities. Lay out the doll on your work surface and check your seams. If you want a symmetrical doll, make sure that you have stitched even seams, especially at the sides of the head, the neck, and the underarms.

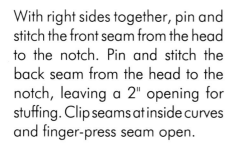

Clip seams at inside curves. Turn the doll right side out.

9

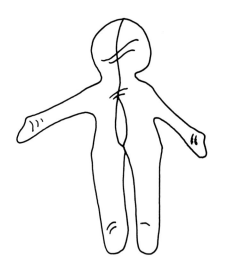

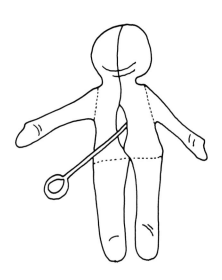

Stuff the hands and feet firmly and continue to stuff to within an inch of the tops of the arms and legs. Stitch these "joints." The doll will be floppier if there is less stuffing in the tops of the arms and legs.

Stuff the head very firmly and then the body. Even when we choose to lightly fill the body to create a soft baby doll, we like to pack the fiberfill to shape the head and provide neck stability.

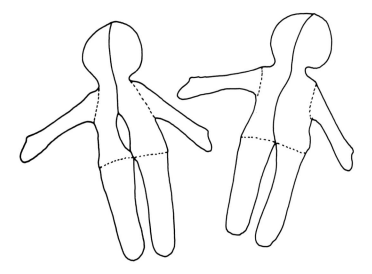

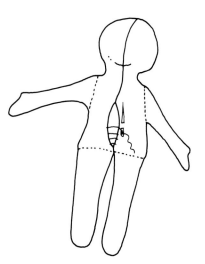

You can vary the angle of the shoulder seam. Narrow shoulders are most becoming on a baby doll because the head appears larger in proportion to the body. Broader shoulders are more appropriate for older characters.

Use quilting thread to close the body with your favorite blind-stitch technique. We like to use a ladder stitch, as illustrated below.

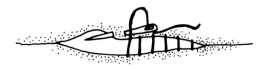

10

DOLLHOUSE DOLL INSTRUCTIONS

These 5$\frac{1}{2}$" and 3$\frac{1}{2}$" dolls and animals are the Dollhouse Dolls in Chapters 3 and 4. Because of their small size, we find it easiest to first stitch these simple little bodies, and then cut, turn, and stuff them.

Trace the pattern onto the grid paper. Create separate patterns for each animal and doll.

Cut templates from plastic or cardboard. Position fabric right sides together. Trace the shape on fabric, aligning the height with lengthwise grain.

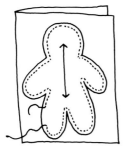

Stitch seams, referring to the pattern for the stitching line at the neck, underarm, and crotch seams. Leave a 1" opening at one side.

Cut out the bodies, just inside the traced line.

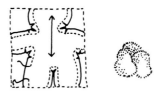

Clip curves. Turn and lightly stuff. Close opening by hand. Stitch at neck and arms by hand or machine. Stitch along the base of each animal's ears, and, on the bear, add a line of stitching across the top of its legs.

Do you see the first signs of your doll's personality? Do you have a baby with chubby cheeks or a sturdy boy with broad shoulders? Did you include the family pet for your group of dollhouse dolls? Now you are ready to apply faces and hairdos to complement your doll bodies. ▪

2 · MATERIALS & PROCESSES

EMBELLISHMENT TECHNIQUES
FOR DOLLMAKING

Experiment with all of the media in your art bin. Pens, paints, dyes, and stains were used to embellish these dolls. The Flower Finery clothes and wings were first soaked in hot water and then partially dipped in dye while still wet to create the gradation of colors.

We like to pin fabrics, yarns, and trims to the dolls' bodies as we plan their hairdos, garments, and accessories. Notice how pins were used to position the features on the dark-dyed doll and bastings were used to create guides for cheek embroidery on the brown dot fabric doll.

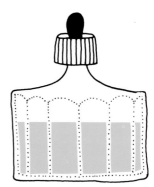

Now that you have a doll body, it's time to embellish it. So gather your materials and start to play with techniques for applying paint, pen, and thread to a three-dimensional doll body.

Dollmaking materials are easily available, inexpensive, and infinitely diverse. Museums display both the charming creations made from the scant materials available in the leanest of times and the elegant dolls of royalty and wealth. You can transform blank purchased or sewn doll bodies into an endless variety of wonderful creations from a few basic craft supplies, fabric remnants, sewing notions, and household linens. Although many of our materials are recycled, we always select high-quality supplies and tools.

Our dollmaking techniques vary from drawing a simple face on a purchased doll body to carefully stitching imaginative fabrics and trims. We enjoy trying out new products and using traditional products in unconventional ways. We encourage you to experiment with your supplies. Explore materials and processes that are unfamiliar and create new uses for old favorites.

This chapter is divided into two sections. Part I covers the supplies you will need. We show how to stock an art bin and a sewing basket for dollmaking and discuss the characteristics of the materials and tools. There is a brief lesson on how to apply the principles of color to your doll projects, and a handy embroidery chart. Part II presents techniques using art, craft, and sewing supplies. You will learn to create skin tones, to design and apply charming faces, and to style imaginative hairdos.

We wish you great pleasure as you explore the materials and processes of dollmaking.

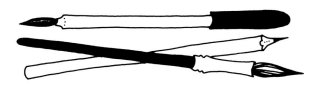

PART I · MATERIALS & TOOLS

We purchase our dollmaking supplies in fine-art stores, crafts centers, fabric shops, and quilt emporiums. In other words, we go to the mall.

THE ART BIN

You will want to have certain basic supplies on hand before you begin to make dolls. Experiment to discover the potential and limitations of each. Test colors on fabrics as similar as possible to the project fabric, because the color on the packaging is not necessarily the color you will achieve on your doll fabric. The more you use art materials, the more comfortable you will be in making choices from the many products and brands available.

We choose permanent, nontoxic, water-based paints, stains, dyes, mediums, and fixatives because they can be washed out of brushes with soap and water and they intermix for great flexibility in dollmaking. Following are the materials and tools we use most often with a brief explanation of how some of them are used. You will collect other art materials as you develop your skills and interests.

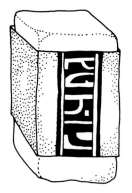

ART BIN CONTENTS

Fabric pens	Brushes and jars
Colored pencils	Sharp scissors
Acrylic paints	Hair dryer
Dyes and stains	Straight pins
Fabric fixative	Sketch paper, pencil, and eraser
Fabric medium	Tablet of palette paper
Cotton test fabric	Color samples or color wheel
Glues	$3/4$" masking tape

FABRIC PENS contain a permanent pigment that can be used on almost all fabrics. Pens come in a wide range of colors with tips that vary in size, shape, and firmness. Extra-fine points are excellent for facial details, while soft, rounded nibs are good for creating blush on cheeks and chin.

Wide, flat tips or long, pointed ones are ideal for filling in solid areas or blending and shading colors. A new pen contains a binder that sometimes discharges and causes the ink to bleed. Be sure to draw on practice fabric to use up this extra binder before drawing on the doll.

ACRYLIC PAINT is pigment in an acrylic binder. It dries quickly to a darker color than when first applied. Full-strength paint is thick and coats fabric, whereas paint thinned with fabric fixative or water leaves a softer texture. Four paints are a must for your art bin—a bottle of Super Hide White by Wally R Company and tubes or bottles of artist-quality acrylic paint in bright red, bright golden yellow, and bright blue. Mixing these colors is discussed in "Using Color" later in this chapter. We do not recommend drawing with any squeeze bottle nozzle; instead use a brush to apply acrylic embellishment paints in glitters, pearlized jewel tones, metallics, and gloss finishes to create interesting accents.

ACRYLIC STAIN is pigment in a transparent base. Dilute with fabric fixative and use to create light, even skin tones on natural fabrics. Stain penetrates the fabric well and lightens as it dries. Stain leaves the fabric stiffer than does fabric dye.

18

FABRIC DYE, a mixture of pigment and additives, penetrates natural fibers and allows the fabric to maintain its original softness. Dyes are wonderful for skin tones and garments. Use dyes carefully, particularly when they are in the powdered form. Each commercial supplier has a variety of brands. Some include a color fixative along with the pigment. Most call for the addition of salt or vinegar as a color-setting agent. Dyes lighten as they dry.

Powdered dyes do not keep once they are mixed with water, so the most practical way to use dry dye for a small doll project is to repackage the dye and fixative into separate resealable containers such as film canisters or tiny jars. Mix only the amount you need for each project in the same ratio as directed for the entire package.

FABRIC FIXATIVE is a watery, clear liquid added to paint and stain. Fixative lightens the hue and increases its colorfastness on fabric. The solution leaves the fabric soft and minimizes streaks when a skin color is applied with a brush.

FABRIC MEDIUM is a milky substance that thickens paint and helps to control bleeding. This is useful when you are painting exact areas of color such as facial features or clothing. Fabric medium makes translucent colors more transparent and opaque colors translucent.

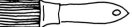

COLORED PENCILS produce wonderfully luminous color for smooth cheek blush and skin tones but use only on dolls that will not be handled or washed. Use graphite pencils only to sketch design ideas on paper; never draw on your doll with them.

BRUSHES of good quality are a pleasure to use and long lasting if properly cared for. Natural bristles are soft, pliable, and hold a lot of pigment. Acrylic bristles are stiffer and are more durable when used on coarse surfaces such as fabrics. For face painting buy a high-quality small, pointed detail brush from a fine-arts store. Also purchase $1/2''$ and $1''$ flat acrylic brushes for painting color onto doll bodies. You will add to these three basic brushes as you develop your painting skills.

GLUES are not advised for embellishing a child's doll. Use glues only on projects that will not be handled or washed. Our favorites are a thick, all-purpose white fabric glue and Beacon's acetone-based FABRI TAC.

COLOR SAMPLES are fun to play with as you plan your doll projects. Collect sample paint chips at hardware stores and lumberyards or purchase a color wheel at your fine-arts store.

USING COLOR

COLOR SELECTION is the first consideration when choosing fabrics, paints, and trims for your doll. Your selections give direction to your design. Play with a generous number of paint chips to explore color schemes as you plan your doll. Notice that light, closely related colors create soft dolls ideal for sleepy times, while bright, contrasting hues invite vigorous play.

Every color, whether light or dark, soft or bright, has three physical properties: hue, value, and intensity.

HUE is the name of a color, such as red or green. Many colors are created by mixing hues. However, the primary hues of red, yellow, and blue cannot be mixed from other colors. These are the basic hues from which all other colors are created. Green, orange, and violet are called the secondary colors because they are combinations of the primaries. All possible colors are mixtures of the primary hues with varying amounts of white or black.

VALUE is the darkness or lightness of a color. Black and white are values, not colors. White lightens a color, and this lighter shade is called a tint. Black darkens and dulls a color. We suggest you do not use black to alter colors in your dollmaking. Black and white are the only pigments that change a color's value without changing its hue.

INTENSITY refers to the brightness of a color. High-intensity colors are very bright; low-intensity or reduced colors are grayed or dulled by the addition of white, black, or another hue. Any addition to a hue lowers its intensity.

EXPERIMENT with your paints to learn the relationship among colors. Squeeze a small amount of one primary and a dab of white onto a palette tablet. Mix as many tints as you can from these two pigments, starting with the darkest. Paint a scrap fabric with these colors as you mix them, noticing the changes in each color as it dries. Repeat this exercise with the other two primaries.

Mix the primaries to create secondary colors, browns, and tans. The secondary colors are made as follows: yellow + blue = green; red + yellow = orange; red + blue = violet. Notice how the color changes depending on the proportion of each hue. Now add white to these secondary colors to lighten them and decrease their intensity. Create browns by combining all three primaries, and mix tans by adding white to the browns.

HARMONY is achieved by using colors that share a common hue. Closely related colors are considered families. Red, maroon, scarlet, coral, rose, pink, orange, and peach all have red as a common hue and are thus members of the red family. It's easy to plan successful color schemes with colors of close harmony because there is a natural relationship among them.

CONTRAST is created by colors that do not share a common hue.

PERCEPTION of color is dependent on its surrounding color. A color will appear more intense next to a dull color and less intense next to a brighter one.

MOST, LESS, AND LEAST is a practical guide for organizing your color selections. Plan your design around three main hues. These can be contrasting hues such as red, yellow, and blue, or harmonious hues, such as yellow, orange, and red. Whichever hues you select, unity is achieved by the careful proportioning of each color. Use one of the three hues as the dominant color, or the "most." The second is the subordinate color, or the "less," and the third is the accent color, or the "least." By carefully limiting the amount of each hue, you can create pleasing arrangements from virtually any three colors.

The primary colors of yellow, red, and blue were used to create the dolls in each row. The hues are arranged from light to dark and from intense to reduced. Very light tints are called pastels. Colors reduced a great deal appear as tans and browns.

Combinations of the primary hues were used to create imaginative color schemes for these doll clothes. Notice how the accent colors appear in different proportions within each outfit, following the "most, less, and least" guideline.

THE SEWING BASKET

It is a pleasure to begin a dollmaking session with tools and sewing supplies close at hand. Following is a list of essentials, discussions on threads, yarns, and fabrics for dollmaking, and an embroidery chart. Add to your supplies as you pursue dollmaking. Often the odd length of yarn or the tiny trim cut from a baby bonnet will be the inspiration for a delightful doll.

SEWING BASKET CONTENTS	
Threads	Doll-body makings (see Chapter 1)
Yarns	Small, sharp scissors, and compass
Notions and trims	Needles, emery strawberry, and thimble
Laces and ribbons	Fine dressmaking pins and safety pins
Fabrics	Long pins with large bead heads

SEWING THREAD is selected for strength and color. Use good quality cotton-wrapped polyester for machine sewing, and choose hand-quilting thread for securing doll hair and for hand gathering.

EMBROIDERY THREADS in assorted fibers and colors are wonderful for applying features and hair as well as trimming garments. Six-strand cotton floss comes in a wide range of colors, is inexpensive, and can be easily separated. Pearl cotton's bulk makes it appropriate for embroidered hair and for accents at the edges of garments. Embroider with wool needlepoint or crewel yarn to create wonderful hair textures. Its sturdy strands can be separated into the perfect bulk, and the yarn is smooth enough to pass easily through a firmly stuffed doll. Shiny silk, rayon, and metallic threads sold on spools for machine sewing are also great for handwork.

YARNS AND CORDS in a variety of textures, colors, and bulk are used for doll hair. Our favorite hair materials have a soft touch and often appear to have subtle color variations. We use cottons, linens, wools, and the inexpensive mystery yarns purchased in outlet stores. We also like rattail and decorative upholstery cords, which are particularly nice for couching in interesting patterns. Each yarn has its own character and can be transformed into many different styles as you experiment.

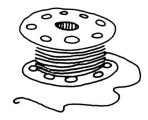

When selecting hair materials, pull on a length to test its strength. Play with each yarn and cord to see its potential when couched, bundled, or braided. Untwist an end and see how the wisps would look on the doll's forehead, or perhaps frizz a length to see the yarn's potential in a moppet hairstyle.

NOTIONS, LACES, RIBBONS, AND TRIMS create interesting doll hair and clothing details. Tiny hooks and eyes, snaps, and buttons can often be rescued from worn garments. Sweaters, embroidered linens, and crocheted baby accessories are also supply sources for your dollmaking.

FABRICS for doll bodies and pattern-related sewing information are discussed in Chapter 1. As you select fabrics for doll clothes, consider the doll's body fabrics, the character's personality, and your sewing skills. Look for soft fabrics that drape well for small garments. Broadcloth-weight cotton and cotton blends are easiest to handle. Avoid coarsely woven fabrics and those that fray easily. Do consider recycled fabrics from garments and linens. Repeated washings give cottons and linens a soft hand and subtle color variations that can add charm to your doll's wardrobe. Shop thrift stores to find lovely cotton scarves with delicate border prints and linen handkerchiefs with woven stripes and plaids in just the right scale for your dolls. Also look for supple silk and lace fabrics in old garments.

NEEDLES are selected by considering your thread and fabric and are kept sharp with an emery strawberry. Use long, thin needles, called long darners or beading needles, to embroider with floss on a doll body. Use heavier yarn darners to embroider hair on a doll. Make sure that the needle has a sharp point and is large enough to create a channel for the yarn to pass through the doll's fiberfill. If the needle is too thin, the yarn will pull out the polyester as you stitch. Test the needle and yarn to make sure the doll-body fabric is sturdy enough. Tapestry needles with blunt ends are useful for stitching knits.

The secondary colors of orange, green, and violet were used for the clothing of these dolls. Each row shows many variations of the same color. There are both warm and cool variations of each hue. This is clearly seen in the row of violet outfits.

We created outfits of secondary colors using accents of both primary and secondary hues. Notice how a color looks brighter when it is placed next to a strongly contrasting hue. Don't be afraid to experiment with unusual color combinations.

USING EMBROIDERY

EMBROIDERY STITCHES are used to create facial features and hairstyles, as well as allover patterns and edgings on garments.

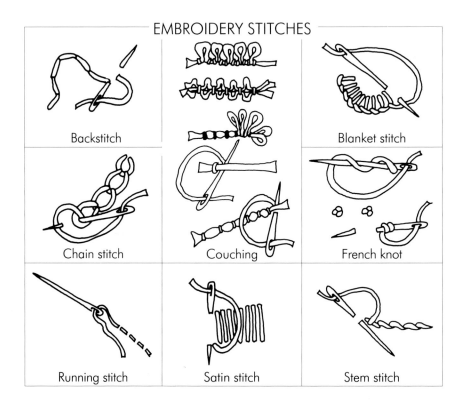

EMBROIDERY STITCHES

Backstitch

Blanket stitch

Chain stitch

Couching

French knot

Running stitch

Satin stitch

Stem stitch

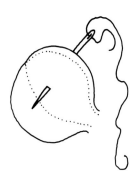

EMBROIDER only on a firmly stuffed doll so that stitches lay on top of the body and do not pucker the fabric. Select a long needle that enables you to exit the doll in an inconspicuous place. Use a fine needle that makes only tiny holes in the fabric. To begin, insert the needle in the back of the doll, leaving the end of the thread visible. Draw the needle out at the location of the first stitch. Anchor the thread with two tiny stitches. As you begin another feature, draw your needle through the fiberfill so that the thread does not become a shadow directly under the doll's skin. Upon completion, anchor the thread with two tiny stitches at the final stitch before drawing the thread out through the back of the doll. Snip the ends of the thread.

PART II · PROCESSES

Here are our techniques for applying the materials to create dolls. We first teach you how to apply skin tones with dyes and stains and then guide you through the process of designing and applying the facial features. Fanciful hairdos complete this section.

DYEING SUPPLIES

Dye	Glass quart canning jar
Salt, as required	Plastic measuring spoons
Brushes	Fine plastic mesh strainer
Rubber gloves	Hair dryer
Glass cup	Masking tape

APPLYING SKIN TONES

If you sew the doll body, the skin tones are created by the fabrics you select. For ready-made dolls, we prefer to create skin tones with permanent dyes and stains, which leave the fabric soft and pliable. Apply these tones quickly, in one even coat. Overbrushing creates streaks and blotches, which are most noticeable when applying darker colors.

We use three basic methods to apply skin tones to all sizes of dolls: (1) brushing dye onto the entire doll, (2) sectional dyeing to define clothing, and (3) machine dyeing for soft, even color. If you are dyeing one doll, it is easiest to brush on the dye, either in an allover color or in sections that define underwear, socks, or swimwear. Machine dyeing is great for up to ten 12" dolls at a time and gives the most uniform results.

Choose the dye or stain. The pigment strength varies with each brand and color, so always test dyes on scrap fabric before dyeing the doll. Here are some of our favorite dyes and the colors they produced on ready-made, natural cotton Give Me Color! dolls. Mix your own combinations of colors to create unique shades. Experiment!

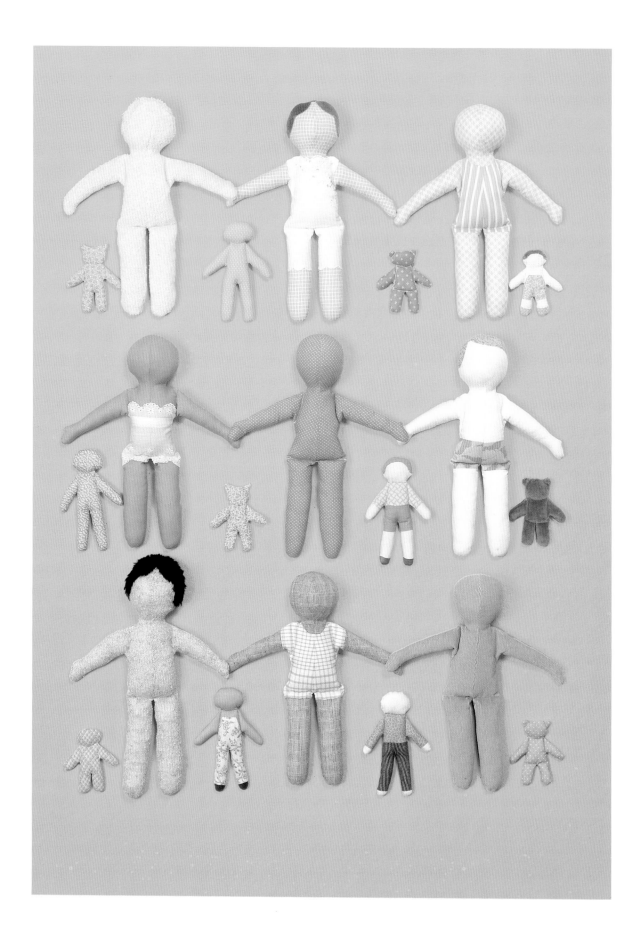

Skin tone is one of your first considerations as you plan your dollmaking project.

Mary used fabrics in imaginative colors and textures to create appealing dolls (opposite). All dolls were sewn from the basic patterns in Chapter 1. Methods for combining fabrics using piecing and overlay techniques are presented in Chapter 3.

Ellie used dyes, stains, and paint to produce wonderfully luminous skin tones (above). She sectionally dyed and stained, machine dyed, and brushed color onto ready-made Give Me Color! bodies. Try all three methods!

DYES FOR SKIN TONES

DEKA L SERIES	
Antique rose	Medium coral to pale peach
Chestnut	Medium brown to tan
Deep brown	Dark, rich brown to tan
Fawn	Light yellow-brown to tan
Mode brown	Medium red-brown to tan
Pink	Medium cool pink to pale pink

DYLON COLD WATER	
Café au lait	Light brown to tan
Koala brown	Medium yellow-ochre to pale tan
Mandarin orange	Dark orange to pale coral
Mexican red	Medium bright rose to pale pink
Nasturtium	Medium warm yellow to pale yellow

RIT LIQUID	
Dark brown	Dark, rich brown to tan
Rose pink	Dark, bright rose to bright pink
Tangerine	Dark, rich orange to bright orange
Yellow	Bright yellow to pale, cool yellow

RIT POWDERED	
Dark brown	Dark, rich brown to tan
Rose pink	Medium cool rose to pale pink
Tan	Medium warm tan to pale tan
Yellow	Medium warm bright yellow to pale yellow

Prepare the cotton body by first clipping the label and then washing the doll in detergent and very hot water if you are going to color the entire doll. Dry the doll if you are going to brush on the color. Leave it wet if you are going to machine dye it. Do not wash the doll if you are sectional dyeing. The sizing in the fabric will keep the painted edges crisp and minimize bleeding.

After you have applied the skin tones, heat set the color by tumbling the doll in a hot dryer for 30 to 40 minutes. To further cure the color and ensure its permanency, set the project aside for a week or two after heat setting. We recommend that you wash and dry all nursery dolls a final time once they are cured to guarantee their colorfastness.

BRUSH-ON DYEING requires the following: package of dye; salt as directed; soft, flat 1" brush; rubber gloves; glass cup; plastic measuring spoons; fine plastic mesh strainer; and hair dryer. Mix a dye solution by adding $1/2$ teaspoon of dye and the correct ratio of additives to $1/2$ cup of boiling water for each 12" doll. Dissolve the mixture and strain. Test the color and adjust. This is a generous amount of color, but it is almost impossible to match the exact shade if you should run out in the middle of your project.

Hold the doll over a sink or basin. Saturate the brush with the dye and start painting on the front of the head. Work quickly to the sides and back. Brush the dye evenly to thoroughly dampen the fabric, being careful not to saturate the batting. When dye soaks into the stuffing, the dye tends to discharge back onto the surface as the fabric dries, causing a blotchy effect.

Work rapidly down and around the neck, the torso, the arms, and finally the legs. Check the seams and any wrinkled areas as you go to make sure the fabric is evenly dyed. Dry the doll with a hair dryer, then heat set.

SECTIONAL DYEING is similar to brush-on dyeing but requires instead a $1/2''$ flat brush and masking tape. First plan a simple garment. Use pins or masking tape as guides but do not draw on the doll. For sleeveless garments use the line of stitching between the arm and shoulder as a guide. Masking tape is a useful guide for crisp sock tops or pant legs, but be careful to brush away from the tape to keep the dye from seeping underneath and smearing. Protect the unpainted body area above each arm and leg with strips of masking tape.

Dip the tip of the brush into the dye and carefully paint the neckline of the garment. Work rapidly up and around the neck to the front of the face, around the sides of the head, and then to the back. Be careful not to splash the dye or overload the brush. Dry the head with a hair dryer.

Now paint one arm. Again paint the garment edge around the arm and then work quickly down and around to the tip of the hand. Dry with the hair dryer before painting the other arm. Paint one leg at a time, drying each as you go. Heat set when dry.

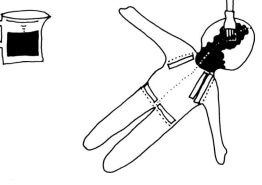

MACHINE DYEING requires one package dye, salt as directed, rubber gloves, plastic spoons, a glass quart canning jar, and a fine plastic mesh strainer. Machine wash the cotton doll bodies in very hot water with detergent. As they are washing, empty the dye with its additives into the canning jar. Fill the jar half full with boiling water. Stir until dissolved.

Remove the rinsed dolls from the washer. Fill the washer with a small load setting of hot water. Pour the dye mixture through the strainer into the machine. Churn a minute or two, then add the wet dolls. Set for a 12-minute wash cycle. Stop the machine and turn the dolls over every few minutes during the wash cycle. Complete the rinse cycle with warm water. Dry in a hot dryer for 30 to 40 minutes.

You can dye up to ten dolls with a variety of skin shades in the same wash cycle by adding dolls every two to three minutes throughout the cycle. Allow four minutes for the lightest skin-tone dolls. The dolls can be put through a second rinse cycle of clear warm water before drying to remove all traces of excess dye and to lighten the color. Once you have dyed the doll bodies, use a hot, soapy wash cycle to clean the machine before washing clothes.

STAINING is done using the same procedure as described for whole or sectional brush-on dyeing. Thoroughly mix the stain with fabric fixative to make a $1/2$ cup solution. Test the color and adjust. Stir the mixture each time you load your brush to prevent the stain from settling on the bottom. Always dry the doll with a hair dryer. If the doll drips dry, the darker colors may become uneven and mottled.

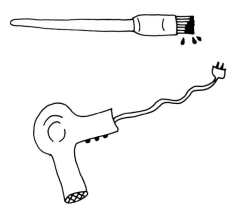

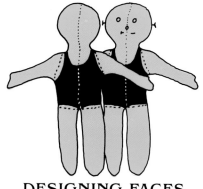

DESIGNING FACES

The face you create gives personality to your doll. We will teach you to plan your face, use pins and tape as placement guides, and then freehand the features with ink or embroidery directly onto the head.

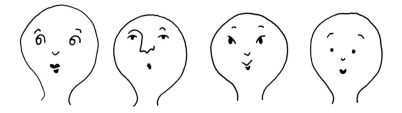

Take time to draw faces on paper so that you understand how the features and the spacing between them create the doll's expression. Notice how the slant of the eyes, the shape of the eyebrows, and the distance between each feature determine the doll's age and personality. Preliminary sketching will also give you confidence in drawing strong, smooth, continuous lines on the doll's head.

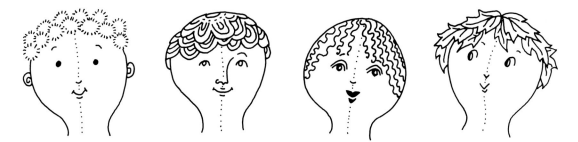

Choose colors that complement the doll's skin tones. Warm, rosy colors accent the nose, lips, and cheeks of pink-tinted faces, and peach shades harmonize with yellow, brown, and peach skins. Keep the color very soft for fresh, young faces. Choose brighter coloring for older characters.

Ellie created expressive faces by designing features of varying shapes and sizes. The simplest face was drawn with black dot eyes and peach pen nose and mouth. The wide-eyed doll at top right has painted eyes, an appliquéd nose, and embroidered lips.

Mary used embroidery for these faces. She also stitched tiny buttons to give bright eyes to the center standing doll and painted the whites of the eyes of the two dolls on the far right. See how the faces vary from stylized to more realistic and how eyelashes can add a perky accent.

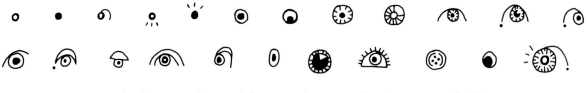

EYES, whether simple or elaborate, begin with a basic pupil. The extra detailing of irises, eyelids, and lashes can be created with pen, paint, or embroidery.

NOSES are often positioned at the fullest part of the curved face. Define the tip of the nose or extend the line to show the sides and the tip. To elaborate, add one or both sides of the nose or draw the nose and eyebrow as a unit.

MOUTHS need a slight upturned line to create a friendly expression. Remember to allow enough space between the top upper lip and the end of the nose.

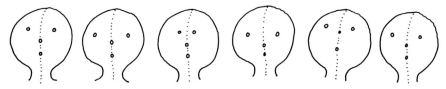

MARK the placement of the features on the doll's head after you have drawn lots of faces. Use masking tape, straight pins, and white basting thread to create guidelines on your doll, but never draw on your doll with pencil. As you work on your firmly stuffed doll, temporary marks can be made by pressing firmly into the head with your fingernail.

Use sharp straight pins to indicate the position of the pupils, the tip of the nose, and the center of the mouth on the doll. Remember to allow for a forehead, chin, and cheeks. Use a 6" see-through grid ruler to position the eyes $^1/2$" to $^3/4$" from the center seam on the 12" doll. If the eyes are too far apart, the face will have a walleyed look. Design the simplest of faces on the Dollhouse Dolls.

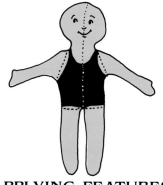

APPLYING FEATURES

Now that you have planned a face and marked the placement of the eyes, nose, and mouth, you are ready to draw or embroider the doll's features. Refer to "The Art Bin" and "The Sewing Basket" sections earlier in this chapter before choosing your media.

PENS in black and peach are used to create the simplest face. Trace around the eye pin heads with an extra-fine black pen to create the pupils. Remove the pins and fill in with black. Mark the tip of the nose with a thin line of peach. Add the mouth with the same peach pen.

A more detailed eye can be created with the addition of an extra-fine brown pen, a pen in an iris color, and white paint. Draw the black pupil, then add a small brown ring around the pupil to outline the iris. Small spokes or notches add interesting texture to the iris. Add the upper eye lid with brown pen. When the brown ink is dry, fill in the iris with color, leaving a wedge from 12 o'clock to 3 o'clock as a highlight on light-skinned dolls. On dark bodies, use paint to fill in the highlight and the whites of the eye.

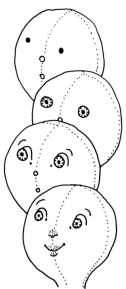

PAINT can further be combined with pen to add more subtle color to the face. Mix fabric medium with your paint for added control. With extra-fine pens, draw the pupils black, and outline in brown the iris, eyelid, eyebrow, tip of the nose, and center line of the mouth. When the ink is dry, fill in the features with paint applied with a fine-pointed detail brush. The iris color can be enhanced by lines, dots, or wedges of lighter or darker color. Fill in the whites of the eyes and add a white highlight to the iris for added sparkle. Paint a soft, warm blush to the top of the nose and define the shape of the lips. To shade the lips, add a thin line of lighter color just below the center mouth line and paint the bottom edge of the lower lip slightly darker.

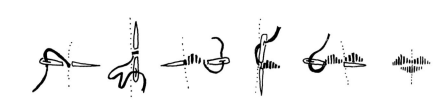

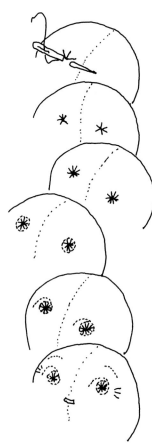

EMBROIDERY is simply done with single strands of cotton floss. Using the pin holes as guides, stitch spokes of well-spaced eye color to indicate the irises. Complete with intermittent spokes of contrasting color. Use a darker thread to backstitch the iris outline, eyelids, and eyebrows. Fill in the whites of the eyes with satin stitch. Suggest the nose with a few satin or backstitches. Begin the mouth at the center seam and work outward to create a pleasant expression. Use backstitch for a simple smile or a satin stitch for rosebud lips.

COMBINE techniques to suit your fancy. Stitch eyebrows and lashes to accent a painted face, or paint the whites of the eyes before you begin to embroider. Tiny buttons make bright irises on dolls for older children.

APPLYING BLUSH
A hint of color is a nice finishing touch for the nose, cheeks, and chin.

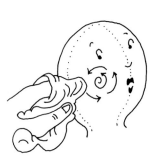

PEN must be applied with a light touch. A well-used, almost dry peach fabric pen with a soft, rounded nib is an excellent tool for light, even blushing. Practice on scrap fabric and then on the back of the elbows to develop an extra light touch.

PAINT is applied in warm shades of peach or pink to create a soft blush. Wrap a clean piece of soft cotton fabric around your finger and moisten the tip with color. Pat the excess paint onto scrap fabric. Starting at the center of the cheek area, lightly rub in a circular motion, lightening your pressure as you rotate to the perimeter. If the circle of color appears too harsh, soften the color while it is still damp by rubbing lightly with a clean, dry cloth. Further soften the color by rubbing in a circular motion with a clean, barely damp cloth. Use a cotton swab covered with soft fabric to apply color to the cheeks of the Dollhouse Dolls.

EMBROIDERY uses the grain of the fabric as a guide for even satin stitches. To define areas of blush, pin paper shapes to the cheeks, then baste around them with sewing thread. The cheeks will have added dimension if the satin stitches cover the basting stitches.

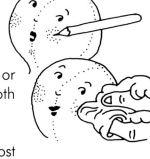

COLORED PENCIL is used only on dolls that will not be handled or washed. Apply a thin, even layer of color, then buff with a clean, white cloth to remove all excess pigment.

DON'T PANIC if the results are not what you originally expected. Almost every face will take on a charming personality of its own, even if the mouth is a little uneven or the eyes are slightly different in size. Save your changes for your next project, whenever possible. There are times, however, when a minor change can improve the face. Look carefully at your doll to see which feature or spacing is not pleasing to you. The following problems and solutions cover the most common complaints.

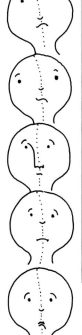

```
────────────────────── EASY CORRECTIONS ──────────────────────
```

Eyes are too high	Increase forehead by placing the hairline at the top seam. Avoid bangs or other dangling hairdos that cover the forehead. Create "big" hair with bundled styles.
Eyes are too far apart	Redraw eyes slightly larger to decrease space between them, or extend inner area of white to bring eyes closer together. Use Super Hide White or embroidery to cover old marks.
Nose is too long	Embroider fringe of lashes along lower eye line to create a smaller area between eyes and end of nose.
Too much space between nose and mouth	Create fuller upper lip.
Chin is too small	Design the doll's garment with a V neckline to create the illusion of a longer neck.

Change the colors in a painted area by repainting with opaque paint or by embroidering. Add Super Hide White to most acrylic pigments for opaque coverage. Do not, however, try to overpaint crimson pigments, as they will almost always bleed through.

APPLYING HAIR

Create a hairstyle to complement your doll's face, size, and personality. Choose a sturdy hairdo for simple crib toys and nursery dolls subject to lots of tugging, hugging, and machine washing. School-age children like dolls with hair that can be combed, braided, and styled. Save your most fragile or elaborate styles for decorative dolls.

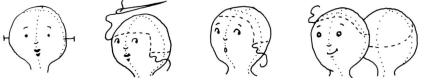

Look at the shape of the doll's head and forehead as you plan a hairdo. Draw stylized designs on paper or pin yarns on the head to see the effect of color and texture. Mark the ear positions with straight pins at the side seam and use white sewing thread to baste the doll's hairline. This is a useful guide whether you are stitching bundles or using embroidery. Use masking tape as a guide to create blunt, even ends if you are going to draw a bobbed hairstyle or bangs.

PENNED designs can be drawn with extra-fine points for delicate patterns or with broader points for blunt or shaded strands. Use lines of varying thicknesses and leave a tiny space between each strand to create an interesting texture.

EMBROIDERED styles use chain, stem, and satin stitches, as well as French knots. Choose strong threads and yarns that are smooth enough to glide through the batting. Firmly anchor ends or loops of the embroidery thread to suggest bangs or leave long strands for braids and ponytails.

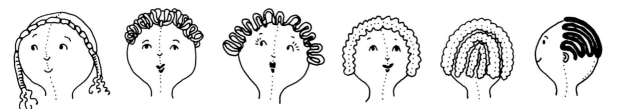

COUCHED hair secures bulky cords or fragile yarns to the doll's head with quilting thread. Follow the natural growth patterns of hair or create fanciful zigzag or striped patterns. Try looping, knotting, or untwisting the yarn between the anchoring stitches, or fray ends of rattail or cording to create graceful curls and tendrils at the nape of the neck, in front of the ears, and at the forehead.

PIECED hair is incorporated into the basic body during the doll's construction. Use the patterns for Pieced Dolls in Chapter 3 to experiment with printed fabrics, as well as velvet, terry cloth, and corduroy.

APPLIQUÉD hair creates durable styles on ready-made dolls. Choose fleece, fake fur, or other highly textured fabric. Measure from ear to ear along the side seam to determine the width. Cut a rectangle 2" to 3" deep, depending on the fullness desired. Place the right side of the hair fabric against the front of the face, along the seam. Stitch in place. Turn the fleece over the top of the head and pin the sides together. Stitch. Gather along the back and stitch the back edge to the head.

Try other simple shapes such as circles and petals for appliquéd hair. Turn under the raw edges if the fabric frays and sew securely on the doll's head. Gather along part lines and hair ends for a three-dimensional look.

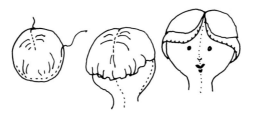

BUNDLED yarn is a versatile method of creating hairstyles. Each style is unique because of the characteristics of the yarn, the length and thickness of each bundle, and the number of bundles used. To create a bundle, loop yarn or floss around cardboard or a few fingers, and then tie it tightly in the center.

The easiest bundle hairstyle uses a 10-yard hank of Needloft Plastic Canvas yarn. Remove the paper cuff, cut an 8" length from one end, and tie the bundle tightly in the center. Clip the loops to form strands. Secure the knotted center of the bundle to the top of the head and anchor the bottom layer of yarn to the crown of the head from the hairline to the top knot.

For a longer, braidable hairstyle, use two hanks. Tie each bundle at one end of the loops and clip the other end to form long strands. Secure one knot at the top of the head. Attach the second bundle directly behind the first. Anchor a layer of hair to the crown of the head. Untwist the yarn, frizz, braid, or gather in pigtails. Trim bangs and sides to fit the doll's face.

Many yarns make wonderful multiple bundle hairstyles. Securely stitch the bundles in rows to cover the entire crown of the head. Starting along the front hairline, sew the bundles close enough so that the loops are held upright by the bundle next to it. These allover bundles can be left looped to form poodle cuts, Afros, and other short curly looks. Cut loops to create moppet styles.

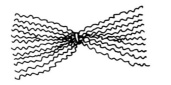

COILED HAIR created from sturdy fringes, rickrack, and braids is a whimsical hairstyle for playable dolls. Arrange a length of trim in coiled rings around the doll's head, always working from the hairline toward the crown of the head.

Lace can be gathered and coiled on the doll's head for a variety of looks, depending on the fullness of the gathers and the width of the lace.

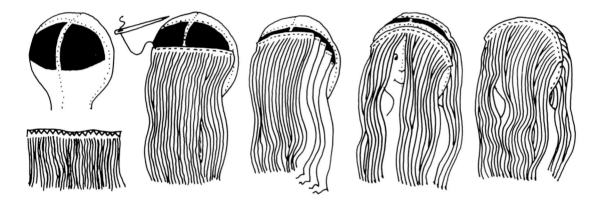

WIGS constructed of long lengths of tightly anchored "hair fringe" can be recycled into doll hair. Carefully remove the lengths of fringe from the wig. Paint the crown of the doll's head the color of the hair. Stitch lengths of the hair fringe in rows at $1/4$" intervals, beginning at the lower back hairline. Reverse the direction of the hair fringe for the front two rows that parallel the doll's head seam.

MISCELLANEOUS items from crafts stores such as pom-poms, silk leaves, flowers, and feathers can be used to create imaginative hairdos for dolls that do not get a lot of handling.

Hairdos of dolls facing forward (left to right): bundled yarn, penned, bundled yarn, recycled wig, French-knotted floss, French-knotted yarn, satin-stitched yarn, bundled yarn, bundled Needloft, bundled yarn, coiled braid, pieced velvet, overlaid knitted fabric, bundled yarn, couched yarn, bundled Needloft, bundled craft hair, couched double bouclé, appliquéd fleece, glued pom-poms.

Hairdos viewed from the back (left to right): bundled yarn, couched chenille, chain-stitched yarn, overlaid knitted fabric, wrapped braids, glued feathers, coiled trim, coiled trim, bundled Needloft, bundled yarn, bundled yarn, satin-stitched yarn, coiled gathered lace, coiled gathered eyelet trim, overlaid fleece fabric, satin-stitched yarn, penned.

You are now well equipped with materials and techniques to create wonderful dolls. Look through the photographs again to see how many different looks were created from a basic body and these easy directions. As you enjoy the projects in the following sections, remember to return to this chapter for background information and detailed instructions. ■

3 · NURSERY DOLLS

CUDDLY DOLLS
FOR PRE-SCHOOL CHILDREN

We chose soft colors for the dyed and sewn Nursery Dolls. First Dolls began as ready-made doll bodies and have simple penned faces and couched hairdos. The added diapers, shoes, and ears were firmly attached with quilting thread. The cat's tiger stripes were penned on a ready-made body.

Pieced Dolls were sewn from variations of the pattern in Chapter 1 in soft terry cloth, warm prints, and plush velvets. Eyes and mouths were embroidered; simple round noses are fabric circles that were gathered and stitched to the faces. Velvet bears were sewn from the modified pattern in Chapter 1.

All of the dolls in this chapter are Nursery Dolls—soft, durable dolls for the youngest children. We used sturdy construction methods and attached nothing that could fall off or be swallowed.

Nursery Dolls are a wonderful way for you to explore the delightful possibilities of the simple doll bodies as you learn dollmaking techniques. You will use the construction and embellishment processes from the previous chapters and will also learn new methods of assembling the sewn bodies.

First Dolls, Pieced Dolls, Tiny Dolls, and animals are either created from purchased Give Me Color! dolls and ornament shapes or sewn from the patterns in Chapter 1. First Dolls emphasize simple embellishments for ready-made bodies and Pieced Dolls are sewn from coordinated fabrics.

All of the pocket-size $5^1/2$" and $3^1/2$" people and animals are ideal for dollhouse play, as well as for traveling with youngsters. Slip an assortment into your purse for waiting rooms and trips about town.

12" FIRST DOLLS

Welcome a new baby or delight a toddler with a special First Doll. These quick and easy dolls begin with ready-made Give Me Color! 12" doll bodies. Assemble a variety of these appealing dolls by combining techniques and materials. Personalize each doll with the features of a special child or tailor the colors to harmonize with a child's room.

Here are our First Dolls. You will want to review the processes in Chapter 2 as you follow the instructions in this chapter.

This playful little girl has warm, pink skin and matching hair. The sectionally painted skin tone defines the unpainted underwear. Shoes are sewn and attached to complete the outfit. Her face is applied with fabric pens and her pink cord pigtails are couched on with quilting thread.

The quickest and easiest of doll projects is this little baby. The unpainted body is decorated with ears, shoes, and a diaper. Two dot eyes and curved lines for the nose and smile are drawn with fabric pen. The topknot of firmly attached pink cord completes this project.

The silk crepe diaper adds appealing texture to this winsome little baby. Follow the exact method as for the unpainted baby dol!, but first dye the skin a soft, cuddly color. The edges of the ears are highlighted with a peach pen. Fray the ends of the cord strands to create tendrils and soft bangs.

SKIN TONES for these dolls are the natural color of the cotton fabric or dyed using the total or sectional dyeing methods. We heat set the colors, then wash and rinse the dolls again to ensure color permanency.

SIMPLE FACES are applied with fabric pens and paint to create lively expressions with just a few details. Add a light blush on the cheeks and elbows.

HAIR is couched securely with quilting thread to softly frame the face. Use sturdy braids, washable yarns, rattail cords, or fake fleece and furs.

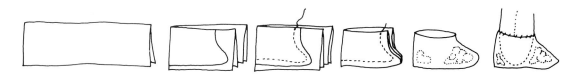

SHOES are stitched from two 6" x 6" rectangles. Fold each fabric piece in half, wrong sides facing.

Fold again, matching folded edge.

Position shoe template. Match shoe top along doublefolds and back of shoe along fold line. Trace pattern onto fabric.

Pin bottom seam of shoe and fit around foot, marking the front seam. Adjust the shoe for each leg and identify the left and right shoes. Remove shoes.

Stitch, cut, and turn.

Stuff heel and toe with fiberfill. Hand stitch to foot.

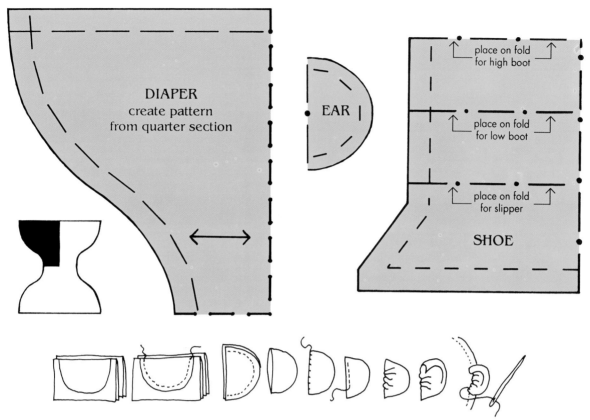

DIAPER
create pattern
from quarter section

EAR

place on fold
for high boot

place on fold
for low boot

place on fold
for slipper

SHOE

EARS for the two babies are created from fabric that matches the doll body. Cut two 3" x 2" rectangles for each ear. Fold each, wrong sides facing, and place two together, matching folds.

Position ear template at fold. Trace pattern onto fabric.

Sew through all four layers, cut, and turn. Hand stitch closed.

Bend, fold, and gather ear into a shell shape. Sew to head along side seam between eyes and mouth. If you have dyed the doll's body, dye ears with the same skin tone before attaching to doll's head.

DIAPER the baby dolls with a soft, pliable fabric. Create a full-size diaper pattern from the quarter section above. Lay out pattern and cut fabric diaper. Position diaper on doll and adjust to fit. Turn under and baste all edges. Pin center back to doll and wrap diaper as you would on a real baby. Hand stitch firmly around all edges. Small safety pins add a whimsical touch, but remember to remove the pins for a child's playtime.

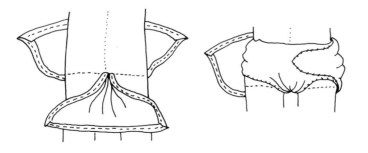

12" PIECED DOLLS

We start with the basic 12" pattern but stitch each doll from several fabrics using a piecing technique. Some dolls have only the hair as the added detail and some have complete outfits incorporated into the sewn body. Remember to consider the stretchiness of the fabrics, as well as the color and pattern of the components, as you create these delightfully attired dolls for the youngest child.

Here are our Pieced Dolls. Use the 12" doll pattern in Chapter 1 and refer to the face embellishments in Chapter 2 as you follow these instructions.

The simplest of the pieced dolls is this soft baby of cotton knit. The pieced hair and the short bloomers are sewn of loopy pink terry. Satin-stitched eyes, a round appliquéd nose, and a backstitched smile complete the sweet face.

Solid and print fabrics are combined for this little girl. Her skin is a basketweave design, and her one-piece suit is a contrasting polka-dot print. Velvet creates texture for her hair and simple shoes. Her face is similar to her little sister's, but notice the different mouth.

The boy is pieced of soft peach and yellow prints, checks, and solids. Velvet gives a nice texture to his hair. The colors of his underwear and knee socks are all closely related to those of the tiny dot skin print. The lively face is embroidered.

First draw the stitching lines for the soft curves of the girl's hair (left). The hair pattern (above) and face pattern (right) have added seam allowances.

Add seam allowances to the stitching lines to create patterns for the boy's side-parted pieced hair.

PLAN your pieced doll. On a tracing of the pattern for the front and the back of the 12" doll, draw lines to indicate the areas for each fabric. Observe the shoulder and leg stitching lines as you choose the outline of the garments. Plan the placement of the facial features as you draw the hairline. Remember that the straight lines of pant legs and waist are easier to sew than the challenging curves of coiffured hair and scooped-neck shirts.

57

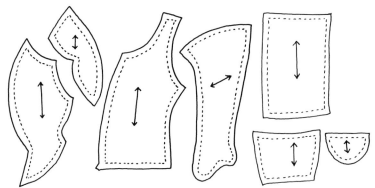

On a second piece of tracing paper, create patterns for each of the fabric areas. Add accurate seam allowances to all stitching lines you have traced and transfer the grainline from the original pattern.

LAY OUT patterns and cut out fabrics. Arrange these fabric pieces on your worktable and play with variations. Cut out alternatives to see the results of using strong or soft colors for garments or shoes. Choose your favorite combination and save the extra pieces for your next doll.

ASSEMBLE each quarter of the pieced doll. Sometimes you must match a convex curve to a concave, or inside, curve. Clip each inside curve. Pin sections right sides together and ease the convex, or outside, curve to fit. Press seams away from the arms, legs, and head sections.

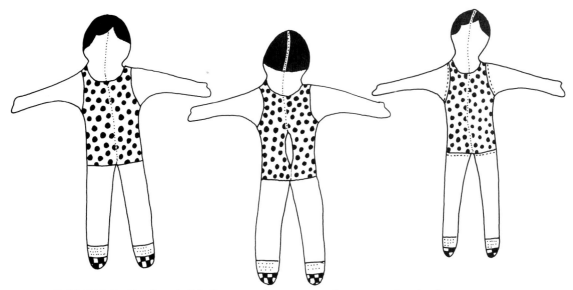

CONSTRUCT the doll following the sewing directions for the basic pattern in Chapter 1. Matching seams carefully, stitch the center front and back seams, then the side. Clip curves, turn, and stuff. Accent the clothing sections with simple blanket, running, or back stitches.

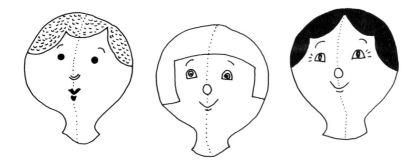

EYES are embroidered. Simple round dots are satin stitched. Whites of the eyes are satin stitched when the irises are rendered in more detail.

NOSES shaped from the skin fabric add dimension to the face. Use a single strand of sewing thread to make a running stitch close to the edge of a 1" circle. Pull thread to turn under the edge. Make a second running stitch around the circle at the fold. Pull thread to create a three-dimensional round nose. Hand stitch onto the center seam. Vary the size and experiment with soft triangular shapes and ovals for your doll's nose.

EARS can be embroidered or shaped from applied fabric, as was done for the First Dolls.

We arranged groups of 12" Nursery Dolls to show how they evolved as we experimented with specific techniques. Differences in the size of each doll's head, slight variations in the placement of features, and alternative clothing details all contributed to developing each of the seven series.

Ready-made bodies were machine dyed, sectionally dyed, or left natural. Many wear dyed ready-made Give Me Color! garments. The overlay technique and piecing were used on the sewn dolls. Those stitched from broadcloth have a crisp look compared to the soft dolls sewn from knitted fabrics.

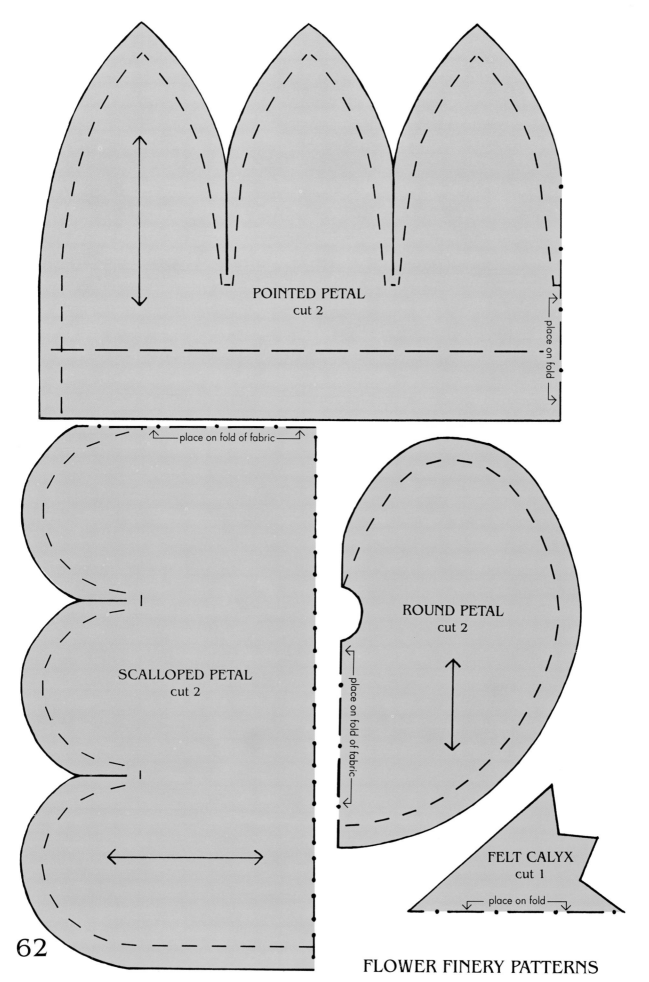

POINTED PETAL
cut 2

place on fold

place on fold of fabric

SCALLOPED PETAL
cut 2

ROUND PETAL
cut 2

place on fold of fabric

FELT CALYX
cut 1

place on fold

62

FLOWER FINERY PATTERNS

SIMPLE 12" DOLL CLOTHES

Clothes help to create the style and personality of your doll. Transform the simple shapes of these imaginative flower petals into many different garments and use the jacket and pants patterns to create a variety of wardrobe basics.

FLOWER FINERY

Three different flower petals are used to create these whimsical garments, hats, and wings, which can transform a Nursery Doll into a perky guardian angel or flower fairy to hang near the crib or perch on a dresser until its young owner is old enough to play with it. Adjust the length and width of the petal shapes to create many variations and finish with bindings and casings. Make templates for your favorite flower shapes.

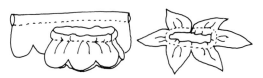

THE BASIC PETALS (round, pointed, scalloped) are constructed from a lightweight, crisp fabric such as organdy. To make finished petals, place fabric right sides together and trace patterns.

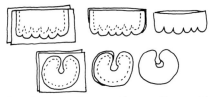

Stitch, cut, clip, and turn. Press. To finish the pointed and scalloped petals, create a casing along the petal's straight edge. All garments begin with a constructed petal.

SKIRTS, PANTS, AND BIBS are created from finished pointed or scalloped petals. Thread casings with elastic and secure.

Stitch the bottom center to create pant crotch. Thread two petals for a fuller skirt. Use ribbon in the casing for an overskirt.

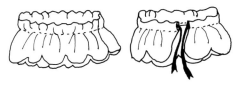

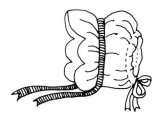

A BONNET is constructed from a finished scalloped petal. Sew a line of gathering stitches across the length of the petal 1" from edge to create a brim.

THE HAT starts with a finished round petal, a felt calyx cut from the pattern, and 3" of rattail cord.

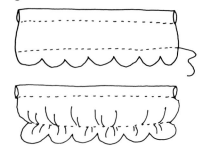

Gather to fit around the doll's head along side seam. Secure. Place a length of narrow ribbon over gathering stitches on the right side of the bonnet. Allow 3" to 4" at each end of ribbon for bonnet ties. Secure.

Gather the raw edge of the finished petal very tightly, funneling the shape to create a cone. Bind the gathered end and secure.

Wrap the calyx to cover the binding thread. Stitch to secure. Add a decorative stem by knotting each end of the rattail. Insert one end into the top of the funneled petal before wrapping the calyx.

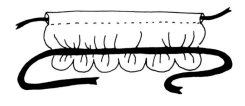

Thread casing with narrow ribbon. Gather to form the back of the bonnet. Tie in a bow and tack the center of the bow to secure.

A CAP is sewn from a finished pointed petal. Thread casing with 12" of ribbon to form the front edge of the cap and chin straps.

Overlap petal points and tack together to shape the back.

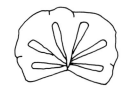

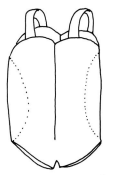

A PLAYSUIT is sewn from two finished round petals and 6" of doublefold binding.

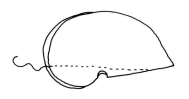

Fold each petal in half. Stitch a dart as shown. Open. Press.

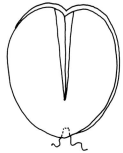

Place petals together, right sides facing. Stitch small V at bottom edge for crotch. Clip, turn, and press.

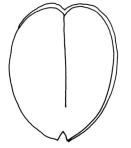

Fit loosely on doll, overlapping sides. Tack overlaps in place. Add straps.

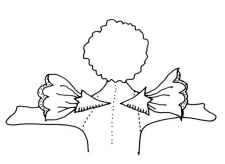

SHEER WINGS transform the doll into a little guardian angel or a cunning flower fairy. Use two long finished petals, scalloped or pointed, and felt calyxes.

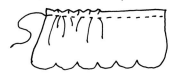

Stitch each petal, but this time do not add a casing. Sew a line of gathering stitches along straight edge.

Gather and wrap, adjusting fullness to form wings. Bind ends with gathering thread and secure.

Attach calyx to cover binding. Stitch two petal wings to the back of the doll or attach them to a garment that can be removed for cuddly moments.

COLORFUL CLOTHES

The jacket and pants are simple, sturdy garments, ideal for Nursery Dolls. Choose colors and patterns that coordinate with the doll-body fabrics. Use the pants pattern to make bloomers with elastic edgings or simple shorts with straight legs. The lined jacket can be trimmed to suit your fancy.

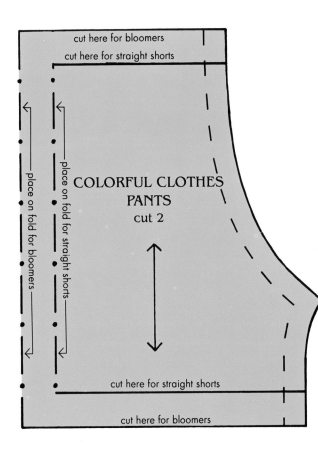

cut here for bloomers
cut here for straight shorts

place on fold for bloomers

place on fold for straight shorts

COLORFUL CLOTHES
PANTS
cut 2

cut here for straight shorts

cut here for bloomers

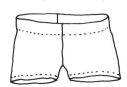

PANTS are cut slim or full. Trace pattern and lay out on straight grain. Cut fabric.

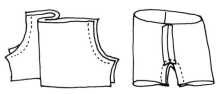

Stitch the center front and back seams, then the crotch seam. Clip curves.

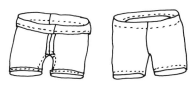

Turn under casing or hem allowances at waist and leg edges. Stitch close to edges.

For bloomers, insert elastic with safety pin and secure.

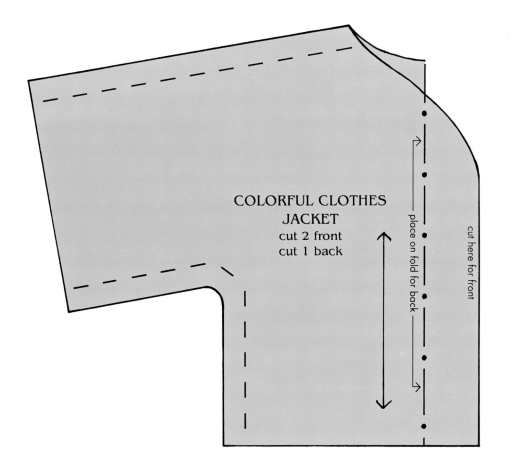

COLORFUL CLOTHES
JACKET
cut 2 front
cut 1 back

place on fold for back

cut here for front

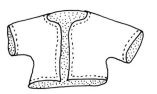

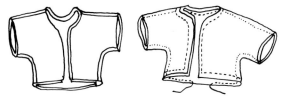

THE JACKET is stitched of two coordinating fabrics. Trace patterns and lay out on straight grain. Cut fabrics.

Stitch the shoulder and side seams for both garment and lining. Clip curves and press.

Position garment to lining, right sides together. Pin edges and stitch from lower back, to the front, around the neck, and to the back again. Leave a 2" opening at center back to turn. Clip curves, turn, and press. Turn under sleeve edges and stitch.

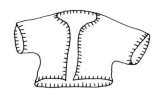

Edge with embroidery or trim.

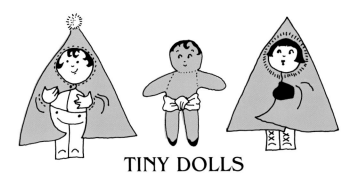

TINY DOLLS

Tiny Dolls are perfect companions for the 12" Playmates. Purchase plump ready-made Give Me Color! ornament shapes or 5½" and 3½" Dollhouse Dolls at crafts and fabric stores or sew little dolls from the basic Dollhouse Doll patterns in Chapter 1.

Use your favorite materials and processes to quickly transform puffy triangles into wizards, puffy bells into birds, and fat Christmas trees into children with hooded cloaks. The 5½" and 3½" Dollhouse Dolls, whether purchased or sewn, are also easily turned into delightful people and animals.

PLAN your doll's face, hair, and outfit on paper. Imaginatively combine these elements as you decide on embellishment techniques. Try a new method or two, as well as your standard favorites.

SKIN TONES are created with the dye, stain, and pen techniques introduced in Chapter 2. Brush on color over the entire doll or in sections to define clothing and skin areas. Use dyes and a washing machine if you are going to color a basketful of Tiny Dolls.

Paint animal fur textures or create striped or calico patterns with fabric pens. Remember to keep these small figures simple.

FACES are applied after you mark the placement of the eyes and the mouth with straight pins. For a penned face, trace around the heads of the eye pins with black to draw little pupils. Add the hint of a nose and a smile with a peach pen, then finish with a blush of color on the cheeks. To embroider, use a single strand of floss to satin stitch dot eyes. Create a nose and winning smile with tiny backstitches.

HAIR, CLOTHING, AND SHOES are added with paint, pen, or embroidery. Create a miniature fairy by crafting tiny wings and a hat.

Reduce the Flower Finery petal patterns from earlier in this chapter or use sections of the full-size patterns for whimsical accessories and garments.

The Nursery Doll Playmates enjoy the company of Tiny Dolls crafted from ready-made muslin shapes and sewn from the Dollhouse Doll patterns in Chapter 1. Dyed First Dolls are quick and easy projects for beginning dollmakers. The seated doll's hat and overskirt were sewn from Flower Finery patterns.

The overlay technique was used to stitch lace panties and socks onto the 12" girl with pieced velvet hair and shoes. Chain stitches were used to suggest sweaters on the Dollhouse Dolls, while blanket, running, and satin stitches; appliqués; pen; and paint were used to embellish the Tiny Dolls.

OVERLAY DOLLHOUSE DOLLS

The hair, clothes, and shoes on these Dollhouse Dolls are appliquéd onto the body sections before they are stitched and stuffed. Use a sturdy foundation fabric for the doll's skin and remember to turn under raw edges if the overlaid fabrics are woven. The finished doll looks similar to a Pieced Doll, but we find it easier to overlay garments and hair on Dollhouse Dolls than to piece tiny bodies. We also use the overlay technique on 12" doll bodies to incorporate fragile fabrics, such as laces, eyelets, and knits, which are not strong enough to be used as pieced fabrics.

The overlay technique is simple. For woven fabrics, appliqué the clothing areas to the foundation section by hand or machine before the doll's construction. For knits, baste the clothing sections but secure the edges after the doll is stitched and stuffed. As you select your fabrics, pull them lengthwise and across the grain. Then, for each doll, combine fabrics with similar give.

OVERLAY PATTERNS

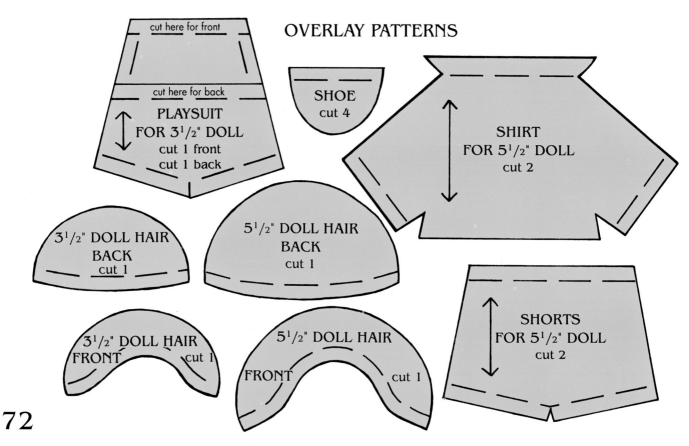

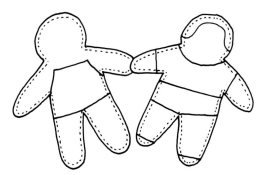

DRAW your overlay design on the doll pattern and create pattern pieces for each overlay area.

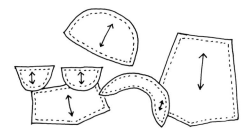

Remember to add hem and seam allowances and to mark the straight grain on each pattern.

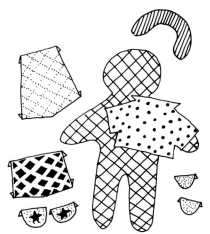

Cut out the front and back of the Dollhouse Doll from the foundation fabric and each of the overlays from coordinating fabrics. Pin and stitch overlay pieces to the doll sections before the doll's construction.

THE PLAYSUIT for the 3$\frac{1}{2}$" doll has a front bib. Clip as indicated, then turn under edges. Press, position, and stitch on the front and back.

SHIRT AND SHORTS patterns are included for the 5$\frac{1}{2}$" doll. Cut out the pieces and turn under the hem allowances. Position and stitch the shirt; then press, pin, and stitch the shorts.

HAIR stitched from fleece, velvet, or other napped fabric adds texture to the Dollhouse Dolls. Cut out the shapes, clip inside curves, turn under the edges, and press. Position the overlays and stitch close to edge.

SHOES are turned under on one edge, positioned, and stitched.

After the overlays are stitched to the front and the back, place the halves right sides together, matching overlays. Stitch seam, clip, turn, and stuff as directed for the basic dolls. Embroider or apply trims to create clothing details.

FACES are applied with pen or embroidery. A simple curve for a mouth and dots for the eyes are charming.

We hope you enjoyed making the Nursery Dolls. Are you surprised at the uniqueness of your doll? As you explore variations, you will see how each doll becomes individual as you change colors, hairstyles, and placement of the features. ▪

4 · TEAPARTY DOLLS

DOLLS FOR THE CREATIVE PLAY OF
SCHOOL-AGE CHILDREN

Our Teaparty Doll Playmates were created from both sewn and ready-made bodies. Embellishment techniques from Chapter 2 were used to create a variety of characters who appear here in their underwear. Dress the Playmates in the imaginative garments featured throughout this chapter.

Ellie dyed her doll bodies, used pen and paint for faces, and created chemises from lovely laces and simple stitch accents. Mary embroidered the features on her dolls and used paint, piecing, and overlays to create undergarments. Enjoy choosing from among the many techniques!

Our Teaparty Dolls include 12" Playmate Dolls and their fanciful 5$^1/_2$" and 3$^1/_2$" Dollhouse Doll companions. These dolls are imaginative friends ideal for the creative play of active grade- schoolers, who will delight in the extra detailing on each doll's hair and face. Older children will enjoy dressing and undressing these dolls in the more elaborate outfits that we craft from the many patterns in this chapter.

These dolls are also ideal for the creative development of dollmakers. As you combine crafting and sewing techniques, you will transform the 12" Playmates and their 5$^1/_2$" and 3$^1/_2$" Dollhouse Doll companions into many different characters. Choose from a variety of skin tones, underwear, faces, and hairdos that can be used on either ready-made or sewn doll bodies in all sizes.

The emphasis in this chapter is on the wardrobes, first for the Dollhouse Dolls and then for the 12" Playmates. Sewing information includes directions for adjusting patterns and some basic construction methods. Traditional patterns and instructions for

creating your own patterns from geometric shapes are then teamed with directions for transforming linens and recycled knits into imaginative garments. Hats and accessories are included to create a wardrobe suitable for all occasions.

For the Teaparty Dolls shown throughout the chapter, we selected party themes as our inspiration. The 12" Playmates are in their underwear, thinking about their plans for the day. Some will play Let's Pretend on a rainy afternoon. They are giving a party for their Dollhouse Doll companions. Naturally, they are dressed in doily capes, floppy hats, and borrowed boots, all worn over their colorful playclothes.

Others will go to a traditional Sunday afternoon birthday party in their crisp dresses and dainty pinafores. These dolls are washed and brushed and are on their best behavior.

A crisp autumn picnic in the grass calls for warm wooly knits and snug hats. We can almost hear the wind blowing—or is it a far away Pan pipe? These cold weather outfits are made from old sweaters, socks, and other thrift store treasures.

Use your imagination as you plan your dolls and choose your dollmaking techniques. Make a whole series of dolls to explore the possibilities of your own ideas. It is through experience that you will discover your creativity and re-experience the fun of playing with dolls.

12" PLAYMATES

Create these 12" dolls from either ready-made Give Me Color! dolls or doll bodies sewn from the pattern in Chapter 1. Embellish them with your own personal selections from the supplies and crafting techniques in Chapter 2. Play with materials in many colors, patterns, and textures as you design each doll's skin tone, underwear, face, and hair.

We experiment with techniques that are new to us as well as use ones that are familiar and easy. Ellie usually creates expressive faces with pen and paint, but she has also stitched tiny eyebrows and appliquéd noses and embroided hair patterns on her delightful dolls. Mary likes to embroider the features because of the comforting knowledge that stitches can be taken out and redone, but she fearlessly paints the whites of the eyes and blushes the cheeks with acrylic color. We encourage you to gradually learn new skills and build confidence in your abilities. Use our dolls as inspiration to create your own special dolls.

Here are our Playmates. Refer to the materials and processes in Chapter 2 as you follow these descriptions.

This simple doll has a bright chemise and delicate slippers painted on the ready-made body. Facial features are applied with embroidery floss, and the cheeks are blushed with a light pink tint paint. Pearl cotton is stem-stitched on the crown of the head and is firmly anchored to create bangs and ponytails.

The ruddy skin tone of this little girl is sectionally painted with acrylic stain. The unpainted chemise is edged with blanket stitching, and the face is applied with pen and paint. Two bundles of untwisted Needloft yarn are attached for the flowing hair. Shoes harmonize with her hair and skin tone.

This bright-eyed child begins with a ready-made body. The machine-dyed skin contrasts with the white openwork of the chemise. Her hair is an interesting trim of loops coiled about the head. Her features are applied with paint and pen. Socks are sewn from the shoe pattern and are stuffed to give her extra height.

The overlay technique from Chapter 3 is used to stitch the cable-knitted chemise onto the warm brown fabric body. The face is embroidered with floss and the hair is made from loopy bundles of chenille. Contrasting yarn trims the underwear and shoes.

This little boy is pieced from checked and print cottons. The engaging face is embroidered with soft browns and pinks. French knots are a practical hairstyle for a busy fellow who likes the embroidered stripes on his undershorts and his cozy flannel slippers.

This little girl is machine-dyed a lovely yellow ochre. Her bright brown eyes and mischievous smile are penned and painted. The hair consists of a coil of 1" black fringe and a crown embroidered with radiating satin stitches. Appliquéd lace forms the underwear.

Teaparty Dolls and their Dollhouse Doll companions on the upper shelf wear playclothes over their pieced and overlay garments. The dainty cape with hood was sewn from an appliquéd napkin. On the lower shelf, the fanciful crown, wings, and Dollhouse Doll clothes were created from Flower Finery shapes.

Crocheted doilies were transformed into shawls, capes, and hats. It's easy to thread a doily's edge with bright ribbon, gather, and secure with a bow to create a charming dust cap. Notice the difference between the soft doily dust cap on the top shelf and the crisp linen one on the bottom shelf.

DOLLHOUSE DOLLS & CLOTHING

Combine construction and embellishment techniques for these $5^1/_2$" and $3^1/_2$" Dollhouse Dolls following the instructions in Chapters 1 and 2. Paint, stain, or dye the skin tones and underwear, or stitch the dolls from fabric scraps.

Apply simple faces using our designs and crafting methods, or invent your own. Finish each doll with a fanciful hairdo. We experimented with wool roving and curly craft hair as well as our favorite bundle and embroidery methods.

For your families of Dollhouse Dolls, create imaginative clothes from our trouser and dress patterns, which are found on page 91. The seam allowances are narrow, so choose tightly woven fabrics. Also look for soft fabrics that will drape on the small doll bodies. Refer to Clothing Tips & Techniques beginning on page 88 for adjusting and constructing methods.

GATHERED DRESS

Attach this sleeveless dress to the completed doll at the shoulders or close it in the back with a snap. Use the pattern on page 91.

Adjust pattern, cut out the dress, and stitch tapered hems at armholes. Stitch back seam. Hem dress.

Turn under the neck edge $^1/_4$" and gather by hand.

Put the dress on the doll and adjust gathers. Tack securely at neckline or secure gathers and add closure. For bloomers, gather the dress at the bottom and tack at the crotch.

84

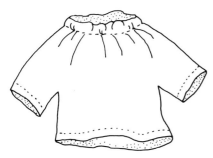

SLEEVED DRESS

An elastic casing at the neckline makes it easy for a child to dress and undress the doll. Use the pattern on page 91.

Lay the doll on dress pattern. Adjust the length of the sleeves and skirt. Cut out fabric.

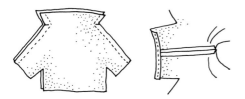

Pin and stitch shoulder seams. Clip inside curves. Pin and stitch narrow hem in sleeves and then the neckline casing.

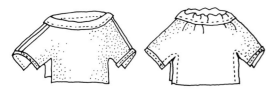

Thread casing with elastic. Stitch side seams. Clip inside curves. Hem dress.

PANTS

Sew bloomers or coveralls from this simple pattern on page 91.

Adjust pattern for length and fullness. Lay out and cut fabric.

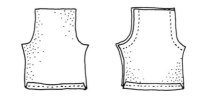

Pin and stitch narrow hem in pant legs and then the center front and back seams. Pin and stitch crotch. Clip inside curves.

Pin and stitch waist casing. Thread with elastic. Secure.

Many variations can be made from these basic patterns. The sleeved dress stitched from a lightweight knit becomes a bulky sweater on a Dollhouse Doll. The same dress stitched from a soft cotton scarf becomes a party dress. Quick, decorative clothing can be made by gathering the turned-under neck edges and waistlines rather than sewing casings.

Each party outfit is unique because of our choice of soft or crisp fabric, adjustments made to patterns, and the selection of trims. The pale coral dress is the sleeveless dress sewn from an embroidered linen, and the cape with hood was made from a bright yellow linen hankie with crocheted lace.

Hats are favorite accessories for Playmates. Two were sewn from the Flower Finery petal patterns and others are variations of the bonnet pattern. The delicate embroidered edges of hankies accent the green and yellow bonnets. Remember to adjust hat patterns to accommodate large hairdos. The wreath is a length of wire-stemmed silk flowers.

CLOTHING TIPS & TECHNIQUES

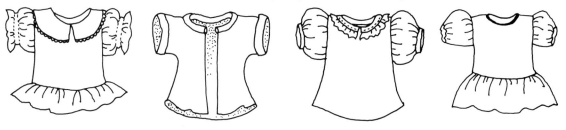

Now that you've created wonderful bodies and made clothes for the smallest dolls, it's time to add hats, dresses, and boots to your 12" doll's wardrobe. You can design many original garments from our patterns, which begin on page 92.

ADJUSTING PATTERNS

Begin planning your outfit by laying the doll on the clothing pattern. As you adjust for length, remember to consider the garment's width. For example, if you simply lengthen the jacket pattern into a street-length dress, the garment will be very narrow around the knees. As a rule of thumb, adjust the fullness along the center grainline and the length at the hemline.

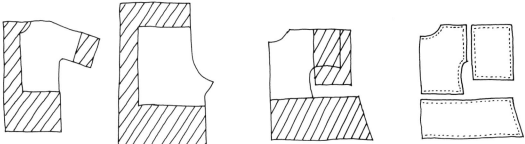

Sections of garments can be altered. See how we changed the long-sleeved blouse to create a party dress with a drop waistline and gathered skirt. Start with the basic pattern and draw the seam, which will join the two sections. Create new patterns with seam allowances for each.

Combine elements from a variety of patterns into original creations.

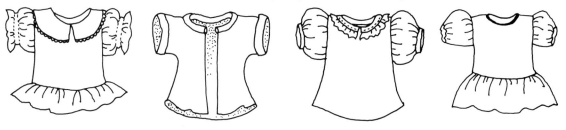

CONSTRUCTION TECHNIQUES

You can make doll clothes with just a few basic dressmaking techniques. Experiment with combining fabrics and adding interesting details.

BIAS STRIPS are applied to curved edges for bindings and casings. Cut from fabric at a 45° angle to the grain. Join bias strips with a $^1/_4$" seam on the straight grain.

BINDINGS are equally visible on each side of a garment. Bind gathered edges to create sleeve cuffs and waistbands or bind linings to garments. Pin the right side of the binding against the garment. Stitch a seam one-fourth the width of the strip. Turn and press the strip edge to meet the edge of the garment. Press at center of binding and stitch by hand or machine.

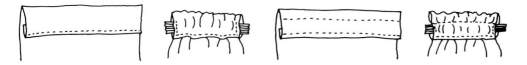

CASINGS are channels for elastic or ribbon and are usually created by a hem. For a decorative casing, apply trims to the hemmed edge or allow extra fabric width for a ruffle. Elastic casings are particularly easy closures for small children. If you use a ribbon, tack it at the casing center or secure it at each end of the gathered casing to prevent it from slipping out.

CLOSURES for doll clothes include snaps, hooks, eyes, buttons, button-holes, and loops.

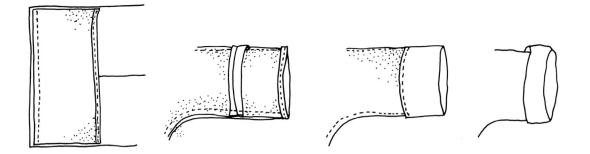

FACINGS are turned to the wrong side of a garment. Cut facing from the garment pattern. Turn under and stitch the outside edge. Pin and stitch facing to garment, right sides together. Turn and press.

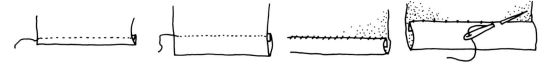

HEMS are the turned edges of a garment. For a narrow hem, press under the edge $^1/_4$". Turn under another $^1/_4$" and stitch by hand or machine.

LININGS create sturdy, reversible pants, jackets, boots, and hats, and are wonderful opportunities to imaginatively combine color and pattern.

Cut and sew a lining the same as for the garment. Stitch lining to garment, right sides together, leaving an opening for turning. Turn right side out and close opening. Another method is to baste the lining to the garment wrong sides together. Stitch binding to edge by hand or machine.

RUFFLES add a dainty trim to aprons, petticoats, and rompers. Hem ruffle edge or fold ruffle in center before gathering.

CLOTHING PATTERNS & INSTRUCTIONS

Use the adjustment techniques and the construction methods to create wonderful garments from these simple patterns. Combine your favorite remnants, linens, and recycled garments to create just the style you want. Then find the perfect rickrack, lace, or buttons to complete the outfit.

DOLLHOUSE DOLL CLOTHES PATTERNS

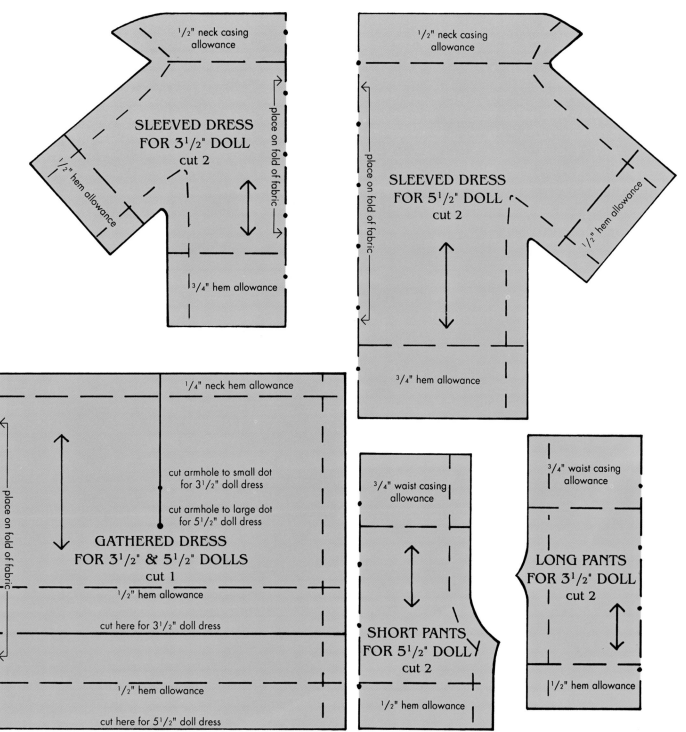

1/2" neck casing allowance

SLEEVED DRESS FOR 3 1/2" DOLL cut 2

place on fold of fabric

1/2" hem allowance

3/4" hem allowance

1/2" neck casing allowance

SLEEVED DRESS FOR 5 1/2" DOLL cut 2

place on fold of fabric

1/2" hem allowance

3/4" hem allowance

1/4" neck hem allowance

cut armhole to small dot for 3 1/2" doll dress

cut armhole to large dot for 5 1/2" doll dress

GATHERED DRESS FOR 3 1/2" & 5 1/2" DOLLS cut 1

place on fold of fabric

1/2" hem allowance

cut here for 3 1/2" doll dress

1/2" hem allowance

cut here for 5 1/2" doll dress

3/4" waist casing allowance

SHORT PANTS FOR 5 1/2" DOLL cut 2

1/2" hem allowance

3/4" waist casing allowance

LONG PANTS FOR 3 1/2" DOLL cut 2

1/2" hem allowance

91

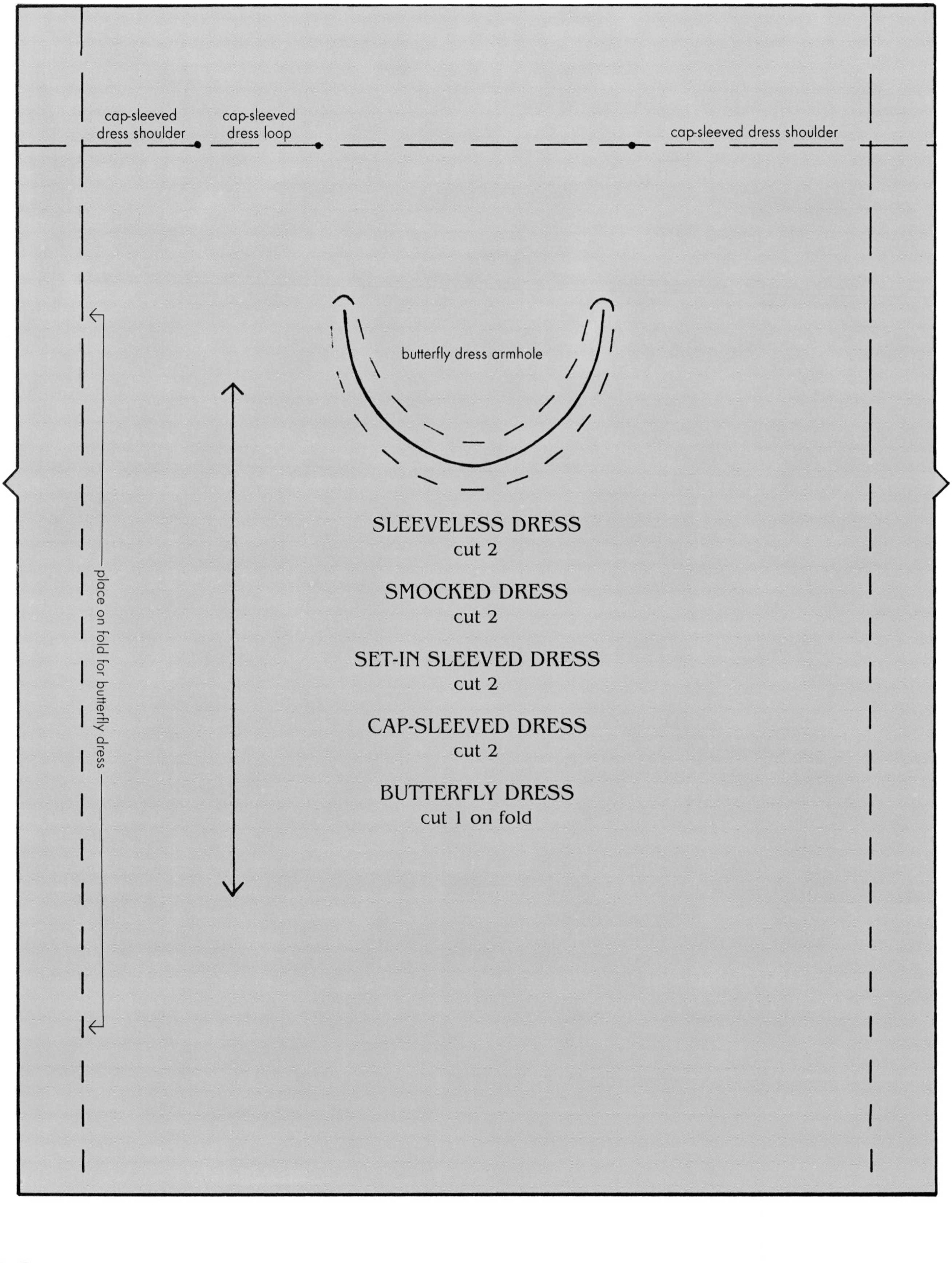

cap-sleeved
dress shoulder

cap-sleeved
dress loop

cap-sleeved dress shoulder

butterfly dress armhole

place on fold for butterfly dress

SLEEVELESS DRESS
cut 2

SMOCKED DRESS
cut 2

SET-IN SLEEVED DRESS
cut 2

CAP-SLEEVED DRESS
cut 2

BUTTERFLY DRESS
cut 1 on fold

12" DOLL CLOTHES PATTERNS

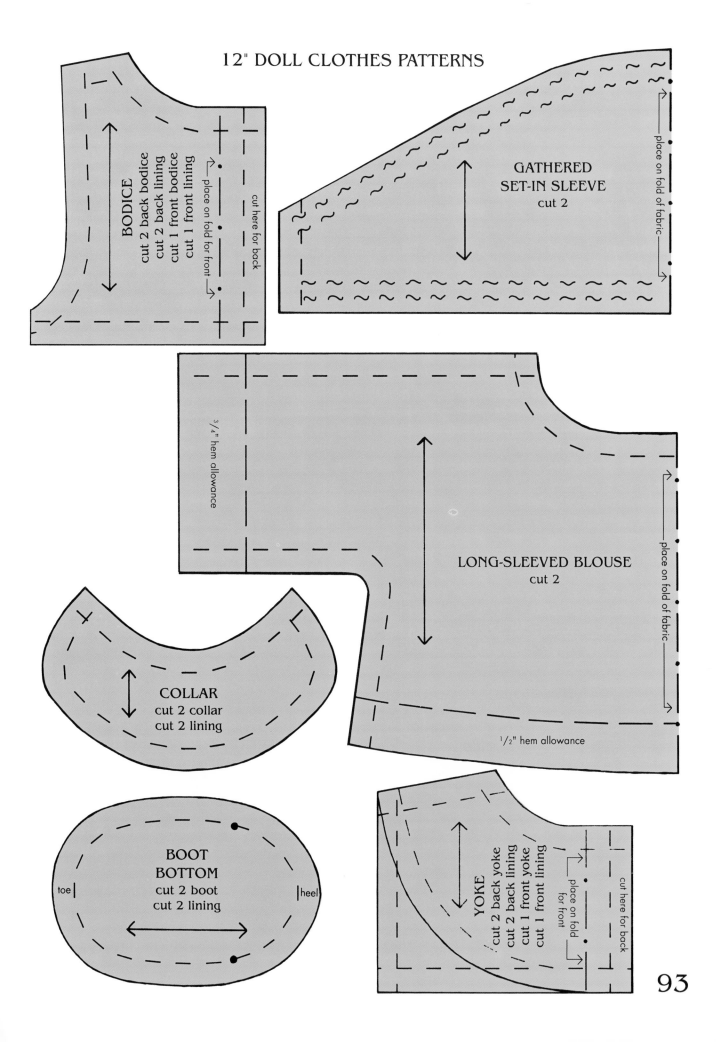

BODICE
cut 2 back bodice
cut 2 back lining
cut 1 front bodice
cut 1 front lining

place on fold for front

cut here for back

GATHERED SET-IN SLEEVE
cut 2

place on fold of fabric

3/4" hem allowance

LONG-SLEEVED BLOUSE
cut 2

place on fold of fabric

1/2" hem allowance

COLLAR
cut 2 collar
cut 2 lining

BOOT BOTTOM
cut 2 boot
cut 2 lining

toe

heel

YOKE
cut 2 back yoke
cut 2 back lining
cut 1 front yoke
cut 1 front lining

place on fold for front

cut here for back

93

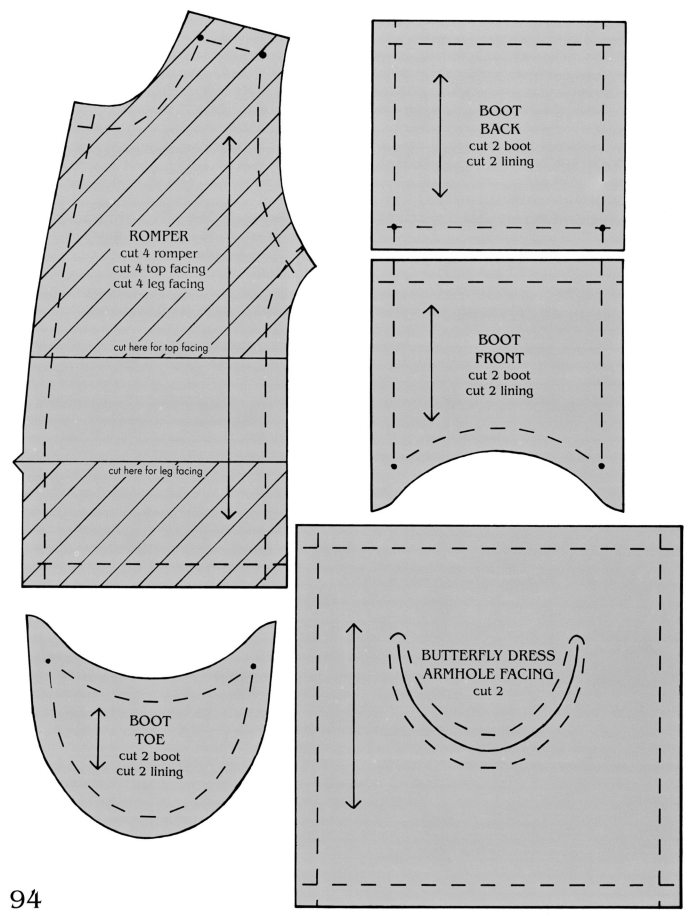

ROMPER
cut 4 romper
cut 4 top facing
cut 4 leg facing

cut here for top facing

cut here for leg facing

BOOT
BACK
cut 2 boot
cut 2 lining

BOOT
FRONT
cut 2 boot
cut 2 lining

BOOT
TOE
cut 2 boot
cut 2 lining

BUTTERFLY DRESS
ARMHOLE FACING
cut 2

12" DOLL CLOTHES INSTRUCTIONS

SLEEVELESS DRESS

Make elegant gowns, playful sundresses, and dainty nighties from this simple pattern. If you bind the gathered neck, remember to add a 2" back opening.

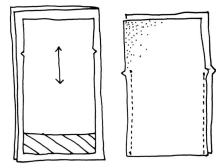

Adjust pattern. Lay out and cut two.

Stitch $1/2$" side seams from notch to hem.

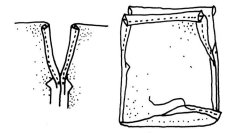

Finish armholes with narrow hems.

Stitch casing at neckline, thread with elastic, and secure. Hem dress.

SMOCKED DRESS

Embroider your own smocking or stitch the sleeveless dress from a recycled smocked garment.

Complete sleeveless dress, but do not insert elastic.

Use a doubled quilting thread or a long machine stitch to create four parallel rows of gathers from notch to casing on both the front and back of dress. Gather to fit across the doll's body and secure.

Embroider tiny backstitches or machine stitch over the gathering threads on right side of dress. Thread casing with elastic for a high neck, or add two straps of self-ribbon for a sundress. Finish straps with small button loops.

95

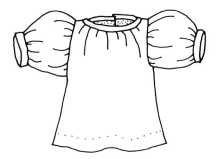

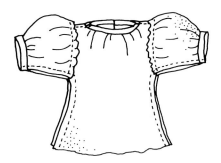

SET-IN SLEEVED DRESS

Add gathered set-in sleeves to a sleeveless or smocked dress. Cut and finish a 2" back opening. Bind the gathered neck edges. Stitch $1/2$" shoulder seams close to edge, but do not sew side seams.

Stitch side seams from sleeve binding to bottom of dress. Hem dress.

Mark armholes $2 1/4$" from shoulder seam.

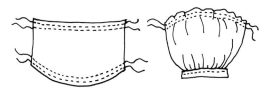

Stitch two rows of gathering stitches in top and bottom of sleeves. Bind bottom of sleeve with a $3 1/4$" x $1 1/4$" strip of fabric cut on the straight grain.

CAP-SLEEVED DRESS

Create another look by stitching the shoulder seams of the basic sleeveless dress to create cap sleeves. Leave a 2" head opening and add a button and loop for a shoulder closure.

Pin sleeves to dress, right sides together. Match at shoulders and adjust gathers. Stitch.

BUTTERFLY DRESS

This childhood favorite is particularly appealing in crisp eyelet.

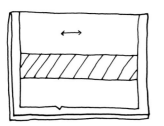

Adjust pattern, place along fold of fabric, and cut one. Cut two armhole facings.

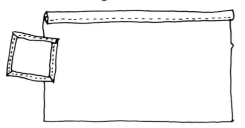

Stitch casing along top edge of dress.

Turn under edges of the armhole facings. Stitch.

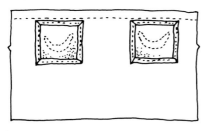

Place squares at armholes, right sides together, and stitch openings.

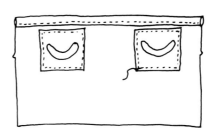

Slit armhole openings. Turn facing to inside and press. Hand stitch edges.

Thread casing with elastic and secure.

Stitch back seam and hem dress.

97

APRON

This simple apron becomes a frilly pinafore with the addition of shoulder ruffles. Decorate with a patch pocket.

Make these patterns: skirt (cut one), 17" x 5"; straps (cut two), $1^{1}/_{4}$" x $5^{3}/_{4}$"; waistband (cut one), $1^{1}/_{4}$" x $7^{1}/_{2}$"; bib (cut one), 2" x 4". Lay out and cut fabric on straight grain.

Fold straps lengthwise, right side out. Press. Turn under $^{1}/_{4}$" along both long edges. Press.

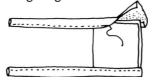

Fold the bib in half, right side out. Press. Position straps over bib edges. Pin. Stitch close to folds.

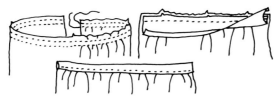

Gather skirt and adjust to fit doll's waist. Bind with waistband. Pin and stitch bib to inside at center front. Stitch center back seam and hem skirt. Cross straps in back. Secure or fasten with snaps.

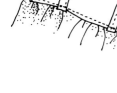

LONG-SLEEVED BLOUSE

Use this pattern for dresses and coats, as well as shirts, in a variety of lengths.

Adjust pattern, lay out, and cut front, back, and a $1^{1}/_{4}$" bias strip for neck.

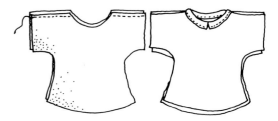

Stitch shoulder seams.

Fold under short ends of bias and position right side of bias to wrong side of dress, with opening at center of dress. Stitch. Turn bias to outside. Turn under edge $^{1}/_{4}$". Stitch to form casing.

Stitch side seams. Clip inside curves. Hem sleeves and bottom. Thread casing with elastic or ribbon. Secure.

ROMPER

Add a bib pocket or contrasting cuffs for playful variations.

Adjust pattern; lay out and cut fabric.

Stitch leg facings to pants, right sides together. Stitch center front and back seams of suit to crotch notch and side seams. Stitch crotch. Clip inside curves.

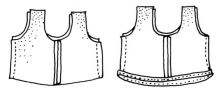

Stitch center front, back, and side seams of top facings. Hem bottom. Pin and stitch top facing to suit between dots. Turn and press. Pin and stitch shoulder seams between dots. Fold under lining at shoulder seams. Stitch by hand.

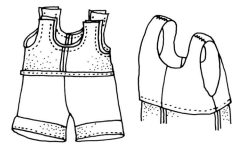

BOOTS

Style these favorites into galoshes, bedroom slippers, or snowshoes.

Lay out patterns. Cut one set for boots and one for linings.

Pin and stitch boot toe to boot front between dots. Clip curve.

Clip heel edge of back. Pin and stitch boot back to boot bottom at the heel between dots. Pin and stitch boot top to toe of boot bottom. Stitch side seams.

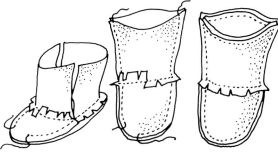

Stitch linings, following the directions above and leaving a 1" opening for turning. Pin boot to lining, right sides together. Stitch top. Turn. Stitch opening by hand.

99

CREATIVE ADDITIONS

Here are three pattern pieces to extend the creative possibilities of the basic wardrobe. The bodice, yoke, and collar all have the same high neckline.

BODICE

Cut bodice and lining fronts and backs. Stitch the shoulder seams of each. Pin bodice to lining. Stitch back opening and neckline. Clip curves, turn, and press. Overlap back opening and secure at waist. Bind the armholes, or add set-in sleeves. Hem the bottom for a blouse or stitch to a skirt or pants.

YOKE

Cut yoke and lining fronts and backs. Stitch shoulder seams of each. Pin yoke to lining. Stitch back opening and neckline. Clip curves, turn, and press. Fold under all raw edges $1/4"$ and press. Finish edges with topstitching for a collar or add a gathered skirt to make a dress.

COLLAR

Cut two collars and two linings. Pin and stitch outside edges. Clip curves, turn, and press. Baste along edge to hold lining and collar together. Position at neckline and baste before finishing neckline.

CIRCLE PATTERNS

Explore the many possibilities of simple, geometric shapes as patterns for your doll garments. Assume a $1/4$" seam allowance on these patterns but always allow for adjustments. Hats especially need to be designed for a particular hairstyle and head size. You might want to use scrap muslin for initial experiments.

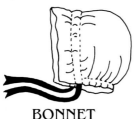

BONNET

This most versatile bonnet is perfect for sunny days.

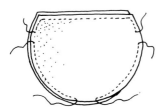

Cut two equal circles 7" to 9" in diameter. Trim $1^1/2$" from one edge, along the grain. Adjust size of pattern to doll's head.

Pin shapes, right sides together. Stitch edge seam, leaving a $1^1/2$" opening at the back and at casing openings as marked.

Turn, press, and stitch opening.

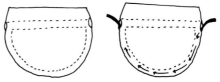

Stitch casings as shown. Thread back casing with sturdy twill tape, gather, and secure. Thread brim casing with ribbon for chin straps.

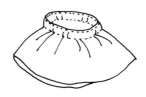

CIRCLE SKIRT

A circle skirt reminds us of bobby socks and saddle shoes.

Cut two equal circles 16" in diameter with a 5" to 6" hole in the center. Clip inside curves. Pin skirt to lining, right sides together. Stitch edge seam. Turn and press. Turn under waist edge on skirt and lining. Pin and stitch casing, leaving opening for elastic. Thread with elastic. Secure.

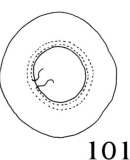

DUST CAP

This easy cap is reminiscent of Colonial Williamsburg.

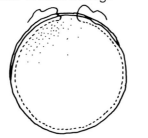

Cut two equal circles with diameters between 7" and 9". Pin cap to lining, right sides together. Stitch edge seam, leaving $1^1/2$" opening.

Turn and press, but do not close opening.

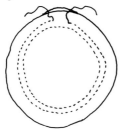

Stitch two lines to make the casing, leaving access for elastic at brim opening.

Thread casing with elastic and secure. Stitch opening.

TAM

Use plaids or solids for this jaunty hat for boys and girls. Adjust size of circle for individual doll's head.

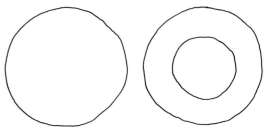

Cut two equal circles with diameters between 5" and 7". Cut a $1^1/2$" to 2" circle from center of one and set aside.

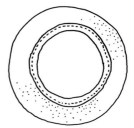

Bind or face edge of the inner hole with bias strip.

Pin circles, right sides together. Stitch outer edge seam. Turn. Press and add decorative loop or pompom.

LINENS

The delicate embroidery and crocheted edges of napkins, tea towels, antimacassars, and handkerchiefs are perfect for doll clothes. We love the exquisite detailing, and the finished edges enhance the simplest construction techniques. We collect our linens at garage sales and thrift stores, where we can find machine-made or partly damaged handmade items for doll clothes. Truly fine handwork is far too precious for us to cut up.

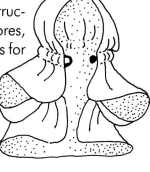

CAPE WITH HOOD

Your pretty 14" to 16" square doesn't need to be cut. Just add a casing and a button closure.

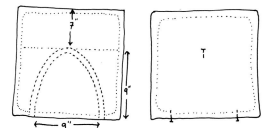

Measure from the center front point and mark neckline casing at center and ends following the suggestions in the diagram. Try on doll and adjust fullness of hood.

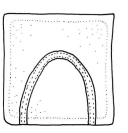

Turn under $1/4$" on each end of a 22" length of singlefold bias tape. Pin ends and center of tape along neckline casing line. Create an arch. Stitch along tape edges.

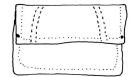

Fold as shown and tack at armholes. Thread casing and add loop and button or hook.

ADJUST your favorite patterns to use the embellishments on napkins, tea towels, and other linens. Position patterns to take advantage of beautiful edges or embroidered corners. Use a single napkin with fagoted edges to create a coordinated outfit of jacket, pants, and top. Stitch a charming tea towel into a sleeveless dress. Use pretty corners for collars. Apply the circle pattern to round doilies to make enchanting hats, capes, and skirts.

The dolls are bundled up for an evening picnic under the stars. Many garments were sewn from recycled legwarmers, socks, and sweaters. We selected bright jewel tones for the coats, reversible jackets, and warm boots. The brilliant blue accents enhance the intensity of the rich, warm colors.

We often adjust patterns as we sew. See how the deep red velvet coat is a quilted, flared version of the basic jacket. The purple cape was sewn from a velvet square lined with a cotton print, stitched following the directions for the cape with hood. The reversible orange velvet jacket has a short bias collar.

KNITS

Transform sweaters, socks, leg warmers, and hats into cozy garments for your dolls. Look for small-scale ribbing and dainty stitched patterns to fit your doll's proportions. Cut your knits cautiously. You may have to modify the pattern measurements depending upon the stretchiness of the knits. Machine stitch with a ball needle, using a straight stitch for seams, then a zigzag to finish the edges. Work drawstrings through the garment with a blunt tapestry needle so that you don't split the knitted yarns.

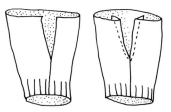

V-NECK SWEATER
Look for the interesting designs knitted into sweater sleeves.

Open the sleeve seam 3" from cut edge. Stitch opening as shown.

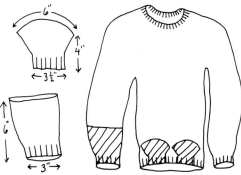

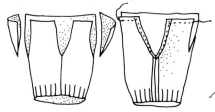

For the doll sweater body, cut a 6" length of a sleeve that measures approximately 3" at the wrist. Cut sleeves from bottom ribbing.

Cut triangles for armholes. Stitch shoulders. Stitch sleeve seams.

Right sides together, stitch sleeves to body. Finish neckline.

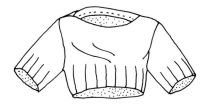

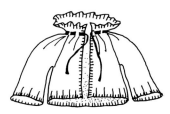

BOAT-NECK SWEATER

A delightful sweater for a summer evening at the beach.

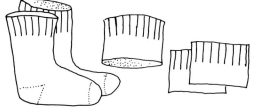

Cut two 4" cuffs from sock tops. The ribbing from one sock becomes the body of the sweater and the other is cut into two sleeves. A longer length becomes a dress.

Split one cuff top to form two rectangles for sleeves. Leave the other as a tube.

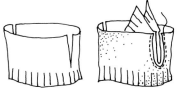

Slit 2" arm openings at either side of tube.

Pin sleeves to fit armholes, right sides together. Stitch.

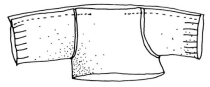

Pin and stitch shoulder seams. Turn under neck edge. Stitch.

RAGLAN CARDIGAN SWEATER

A pullover sweater can also be made with this technique.

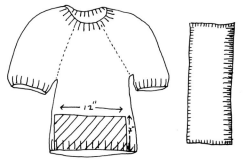

Cut ribbing 12" wide x 7" long. Finish edges with blanket stitch.

Fold right sides together and baste 2" sleeve and side seams. Stitch, allowing $3/8$" between sleeve seam stitches and side stitches. Try sweater on doll.

Cut underarms and zigzag edges. Try sweater on doll to pin darts. Stitch darts. Thread cord $1/2$" from edge to create a soft collar.

107

RECYCLED GARMENTS

Your family's favorite outgrown clothes or thrift store finds present unlimited possibilities for doll clothes. Transform a delicate collar from an infant's dress into a sun brim with a ribbon tie. The brim becomes a hat with the addition of a circle crown. Use a puffy elasticized sleeve to create a dust cap or sew two bound sleeves from an infant's dress into bloomers. The placket with tiny buttons can even be the closure on your doll's garment. Add a casing to a ready-made collar to craft a frilly skirt or cape.

Many imaginative accessories are created from recycled knits. One wooly sock becomes three different hats: a snug cap from the toe, a ski hood from the heel, and a ribbed snow hat from the sock top. Make other headgear, dickies, tights, stockings, and shoes, from sweaters and leg warmers.

Each time you create dolls and clothing from these basic directions, patterns, and construction techniques, you will get new ideas. As you gain confidence in your skills, use thoughts of other times and make-believe places to inspire your next doll project. ▪

CONCLUSION · A FAIRY TALE ENDING

For our final presentation we chose to design dolls for the pure pleasure of playing with colors and textures. Without observing the safety concerns of children's toys, we worked within the fantasy theme of Elfin Folk as we selected from our favorite materials and techniques.

Spring and her attendants alight through the window to bring brilliant color to a sleeping city. Summer harvests the last flower hat of the season while Autumn Oak and Thistle play with their little sprite companions amid falling leaves and drying grasses.

Mary found Spring's fragile cotton voile in a charming '40s apron. She instantly recognized that the leafy patterned fabric would be a flowing gown for the Harbinger of Spring and incorporated the apron's ruffled edge and pockets into the graceful garment. She discovered the tiny ringlet hair when she inadvertently pulled apart a bouclé yarn. Hairdos for the little sprites include tight French knots in needlepoint wool, loopy bundles of fine crochet thread, and a few clipped bundles of variegated cotton as a topknot on the smallest doll.

Ellie dyed Summer's Flower Finery garments in soft gradations of color and sewed her high boots from an embroidered napkin. Autumn Oak wears a velvet tunic and an acorn cap that was crafted from an enlarged head segment of the 12" doll pattern. Thistle's dress was assembled from a length of cotton fringe and snippets of brown felt. Her glittery wings were easily constructed from wired ribbon, twisted into shape, and tacked with quilting thread.

Throughout the book, we have shared with you our methods and materials for making playable dolls for the children in your life. We encourage you to use these same techniques to create the characters of your fantasies. Thank you for creating and crafting dolls with us. We have many corners of our imaginations yet to visit and perhaps we will meet you there. ▪

INDEX

C: Color Photo P: Pattern

OTHER BOOKS AVAILABLE FROM CHILTON
Robbie Fanning, Series Editor